the SERGER IDEA BOOK

A COLLECTION OF INSPIRING IDEAS FROM THE PALMER/PLETSCH PROFESSIONALS

Compiled and written by Ann Hesse Price
Edited by Pati Palmer

Book design, production and editorial assistance by Linda Wisner

Technical illustrations by Kate Pryka
Fashion photography by Carole Meyer assisted by Kim Meyer
Accessories by Cleo Cummings
Cover garment by Marta Alto
Cover photo by Charles True
Identification photography by Pati Palmer
assisted by Kathleen Spike and Marta Alto

This book is dedicated to Pati Palmer's husband Jack Watson for allowing their home to be in chaos for several months with racks of clothes and accessories, book meetings and 18-hour days on the computer AND for being both mother and father to their daughter Melissa for the last 6 months. Also to 3-year old Melissa for her patience.

A special thanks to Lynette Ranney Black, Palmer/Pletsch Promotions Manager, for keeping the office, seminars, workshops, communications, and this project, going. And thanks to Ron Ellwanger and Jeff Watson for taking charge of the rest of the business while we were all so involved.

More thanks to others who helped us out...Jerry Fellows, Marla Kazel, Kelley Salber, Rhoda Elliott, all sewing machine companies and thread manufacturers, the McCall Pattern Company, Harrison Typesetting, Inc., Graphic Color/Portland Prep Center, Craftsman Press, Jerry Alto and Stacy Alto.

We all thank Linda Wisner's husband Bill Day for his patience and support as she worked night and day on this book for the last several months.

Whenever brand names are mentioned, it is only to indicate to the consumer products which we have personally tested and with which we have been pleased. It is also meant to save our students time. There may be further products that are comparable to aid you in your sewing.

Foreword: A Message from Pati Palmer...

Having been in the home sewing industry since 1969, I've seen many changes. My first job was with The Armo Co., a shaping fabrics manufacturer, as one of 30 educational representatives. The industry employed 200 home economists who provided *free* education.

When business slacked off during the early 1970's, many of these jobs were eliminated. It did not help matters that the industry was also fragmented. At that time I was a notions buyer for a department store. With limited travel funds I was asked to decide which trade shows to attend, the notions shows or the fabric shows.

The American Home Sewing Association was established in 1977 in New York City and combined two of the trade associations, The National Notions Association established in 1928, and the American Home Sewing Council established in 1969. Today, AHSA has over 300 members who are manufacturers, publishers, retailers, and educators. For membership information and for educational materials, write to them at 1375 Broadway, New York, N.Y. 10018. The $25 educator membership fee includes trade show information and the quarterly *Inside AHSA* newsletter.

With support from its membership, the Association has sponsored the development of the American Sewing Guild from two test cities in 1978 to over 70 chapters in all 50 states today. Composed of sewing enthusiasts who banded together to learn more about sewing, the Guilds continue to grow. For information on starting or joining a guild write The American Sewing Guild, P.O. Box 50936, Indianapolis, Indiana 46250.

Best of all, the industry has entered an era of new technology, with the SERGER being the most important development. Sewers and non-sewers alike are fascinated, and sales have skyrocketed. News releases on the latest sewing technology have been picked up by newspapers throughout the country. As a result, people are talking about sewing again!

In 1985, Palmer/Pletsch Associates produced *Sewing With Sergers* to tell everyone what a serger is and how to use it. Soon after, we began conducting four-day, hands-on serger workshops in Portland, Oregon, and found our students *wanted* to use their sergers for instant creativity as well. To answer that need, we published *Creative Serging*. That book only whetted their appetite. Color photography was requested. *The Serger Idea Book* was born.

This is a book that no single individual could have written. Some of our inspiration came from our many workshop graduates, while the actual garments you see in this book are the work of our Associates. Together we created more than 300 pieces, testing ideas to bring you the best.

We hope you'll enjoy this "coffee table" sewing book. For more in-depth information on serging, please consult our other two serger books. They don't have the same "gift book look," but you will find them jam-packed with information!

HAPPY SEWING!

Pati Palmer

Pati Palmer

ABOUT THE CONTRIBUTORS

Collectively, these fashion sewing authorities have been making their own clothes for over 189 years and have been employed in the sewing industry for over 106 years! They have conducted over a thousand seminars and workshops in every state from Maine to Hawaii and from Alaska to Florida; in every province of Canada; and Pati has even made presentations in Australia! And they don't limit themselves to just the fashion capitals either. Palmer/Pletsch Associates have ventured more than once to lecture and demonstrate to groups in Iola, Kansas; Tazewell, Virginia; Willmar, Minnesota; and Chelan, Washington. You know what that means.... They can tell you where the best fabric stores are (though they have nothing to complain about in their headquarters of Portland, Oregon!) **and** where you'll find the best selection of serger threads.

The Palmer/Pletsch Professionals (from left): Linda Wisner, Lynn Raasch, Marta Alto, Pati Palmer, Kathleen Spike, Karen Dillon and Ann Price.

Each of the Palmer/Pletsch professionals can point to individual accomplishments as well.

Pati Palmer, owner of Palmer/Pletsch Associates, spends most of her time overseeing and contributing to the many areas of her company, including the book publishing, Trends Bulletins, notions, and promotions divisions. Pati used to travel 26 weeks a year teaching seminars but since 1986 her new daughter has slowed her down. Pati still speaks by invitation occasionally throughout North America and in Australia. With Susan Pletsch, she has written innovative guide sheets and designed nearly 100 patterns for the McCall Pattern Company. Before starting Palmer/Pletsch in 1974, Pati was a retail buyer, a department store home economist and an educational representative for an interfacing manufacturer. A graduate of Oregon State University, she is a Certified Home Economist, and active on the national board of Home Economists in Business.

Ann Price, publications coordinator for Palmer/Pletsch, has conducted serger workshops throughout the U.S. and authored the Trends Bulletin on decorative threads. In addition, she writes two monthly columns for **Sew News** magazine. Ann is a Certified Home Economist with a degree from Oregon State University. Most recently, she was corporate educational manager for Bernina sewing machines. She wrote their first supplemental serger manual and worked as educational liaison to the parent company in Switzerland.

Linda Wisner, marketing director for Palmer/Pletsch, is responsible for advertising and promotion of all Palmer/Pletsch products. She has owned an advertising agency since 1979, and her clients have included many companies in the home-sewing industry. Wisner Associates has received regional and national awards for newspaper advertising, logo design, packaging, direct mail and letterhead designs. Linda holds a B.A. degree from Macalester College in Minnesota and did graduate work in advertising, journalism and design at the University of Minnesota and the Minneapolis College of Art and Design.

Marta Alto's sewing experience stems from her study of home economics at Oregon State University, combined with several seasons sewing costumes for the Oregon Shakespearean Festival. During the past 15 years, Marta has enjoyed an active career teaching others her no-nonsense approach to sewing at a major department store, fabric stores and for Palmer/Pletsch. While she holds the distinction of being the Palmer/Pletsch Ultrasuede® expert (She co-authored our Trends Bulletin on the subject), she conducts seminars on all topics throughout North America. In addition, she has been involved with the serger workshops in Portland from their start in 1985.

Karen Dillon graduated with a Clothing/Textiles in Business degree from Montana State University and has been in the fashion/sewing industry ever since—in retail sales with large department stores; as an educational representative and supervisor for the Armo Company, a shaping fabrics manufacturer; and as the sewing consultant for New York Fabrics near San Francisco. She has traveled throughout North America during her many years as an educational representative for Palmer/Pletsch. In 1980 she co-authored **Sew a Beautiful Wedding** and is featured in our "Welcome to My Sewing Room" video, **Sewing Today the Timesaving Way**.

Lynn Raasch has traveled the U.S. and Canada as a consumer education specialist most of her career—for Maytag, Johnson Wax, the Florida lime and avocado industry and the California Strawberry Advisory Board. Since joining Palmer/Pletsch in 1983, she has conducted seminars and workshops "on the road" as well as the four-day, hands-on serger workshops in Portland. She is also featured in our video, **Sewing Today the Timesaving Way**. Lynn earned her home economics degree at the University of Wisconsin–Stout, where she majored in clothing, textiles and design. A lifetime fashion-sewer, Lynn loves the challenge of trying something innovative with each new fabric and design.

Kathleen Spike joined Palmer/Pletsch just in time to become involved with the development of this book! She has owned a custom dressmaking business in Portland for 15 years and was the founder of the Custom Clothing Guild of Oregon in 1984. She shares her business "secrets" in the Palmer/Pletsch book and video, **Sew to Success!** Kathy also owns and operates a contemporary sewing school, and has co-authored the book **Fast Fashion Jeans for Family Fun**. She is teaching workshops and seminars for Palmer/Pletsch throughout the United States and Canada.

TABLE OF CONTENTS

 # *Welcome* TO THE WORLD OF SERGING

The initial working title of this book was, "THE CREATIVE SERGER IDEA BOOK," but then we thought — that's not really the whole point. After all, a serger is valuable for so much IN ADDITION TO decorative applications. While a serger does open a whole new world of (sophisticated) creativity for the home- sewer, it is also a machine that enables one to sew more in less time, with more professional results.

Many serger owners use their machines for nothing more than finishing edges, just as many microwave oven owners use that appliance for nothing more than warming leftovers. THERE IS NOTHING WRONG WITH THAT. You have probably already decided the serger was worth the investment just to be able to speed up that otherwise tedious process of edge finishing and to provide a professional look at the same time.

But this compact machine can do so much more, as you learned when you read our basic book, SEWING WITH SERGERS. Its "sequel," CREATIVE SERGING, goes into more depth on decorative overlock sewing, but READ ON! We're going to show you pages and pages of tried-and-tested ideas for enjoying the full versatility of your serger. And we'll tell you the decision making that went into creating each project. Once you see how easy and fun it can be to use serger methods, you'll be thinking of ways to adapt all of your sewing projects to incorporate your serger more.

Some of the entries in the book will demonstrate practical applications, and many will show you decorative possibilities. Since pattern companies cannot include all the serging options for EACH design, you can adapt the techniques we've used to create similar looks. Read our directions then EXPERIMENT! to find what's best for *your* garments. There is NO RIGHT OR WRONG—it's what works!

We saw this designer suit in a magazine. It was actually white leather appliqued with narrow strips of black leather.

It inspired us to develop the "random yarn" technique used on this sweatshirt. We flatlocked yarn to the fabric using clear nylon thread. (See page 32 for our technique.)

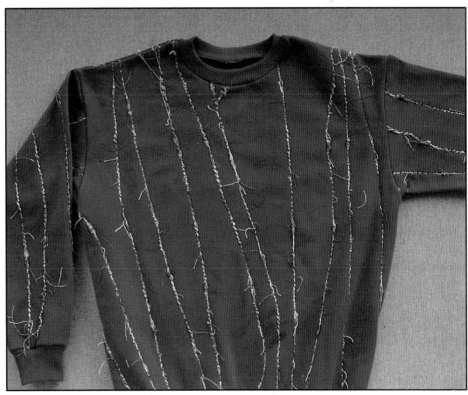

SERGERS HAVE IMPROVED

Pictured below are representative models from each of the major serger importers. Just like any other appliance, sergers become more and more advanced as technological developments make that possible. This is GOOD NEWS! It may be disappointing to learn, six months after you bought your serger, that a "new and improved" version is now available; but where would we be without the improvements we've seen in just the last five years? After all, with all the advances, sergers are now easier to use and more versatile than ever.

Before you think you should have "waited" for the newest model, just think of how much you've enjoyed using your serger in the meantime. There will always be a "newer" model — and you don't want to wait till eternity! If you decide to upgrade, you'll probably find a buyer who would love a good used model at a good price. Or, consider keeping it — We would! Today's luxury sewing room has TWO sergers! Set one up for regular seaming and one for a rolled edge. For decorative serging, two sergers will cut your time in half. Serge seams on one with regular thread, and do your decorative work on the other without having to rethread the machine and readjust tensions.

needle

stitch finger

upper looper

knife

lower looper

SERGER BASICS

A serger trims, stitches, then totally encases the edge of fabric with thread. It not only prevents raveling, but also provides a neatly finished look inside a garment. Because stitches are formed over a metal **stitch finger**, the edge doesn't draw up, even on lightweight silkies.

Because a serger's *"loopers"* go OVER AND UNDER rather than through the fabric, you can use heavy threads, yarns and ribbons for decorative effects. The specialty thread need not fit into the needle.

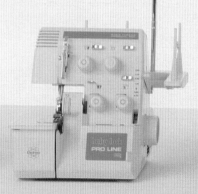

A "GENERIC SERGER"

Review the main parts of a serger in this drawing of a 3/4-thread model, the most common. By contrast, a 3-thread machine has only one needle and three tension dials, while a 5-thread model has two needles plus another lower looper and tension dial. A 2-thread serger has only one needle, one looper and two tension dials.

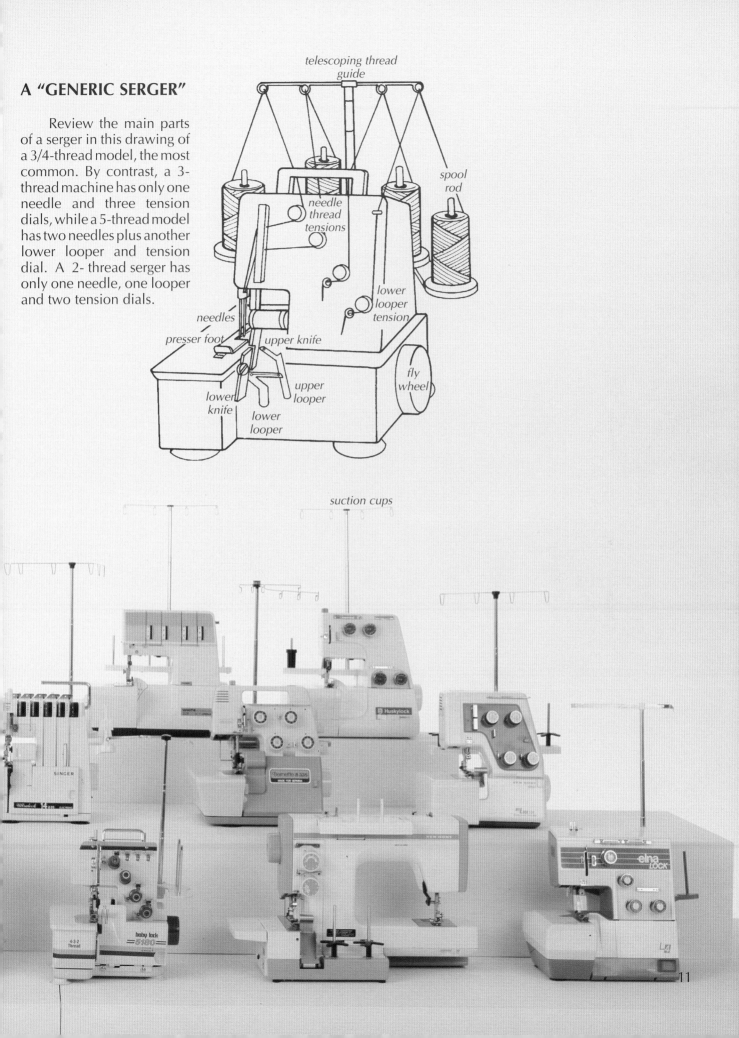

telescoping thread guide

spool rod

needle thread tensions

lower looper tension

needles

presser foot

upper knife

lower knife

upper looper

lower looper

fly wheel

suction cups

11

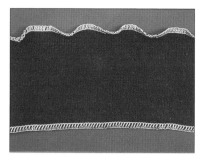

Without differential feed, sweaterknits stretch; with differential feed set on 2, no stretching occurs.

Without differential feed, silkies can pucker; with differential feed set on 0.7, no puckering occurs.

DIFFERENTIAL FEED

All sewing machines and sergers have feed dogs, metal "teeth," that come up through the throat plate, grab the fabric and move it along. Many sergers now feature DIFFERENTIAL feed, meaning the machine has two sets of feed dogs equipped to work at different rates if necessary. When the dial is set on 1 for normal feeding, the feed dogs move at the same rate.

But if the dial is set on 2, the front feed dog takes in twice as much fabric under the presser foot as the rear feed dog releases. The result is similar to a technique called "ease-plussing" (placing your finger behind the presser foot to restrict feeding). This setting is used on sweaterknits to prevent stretching which causes wavy seams. On non-stretchy fabrics, it could cause puckering or even gathering.

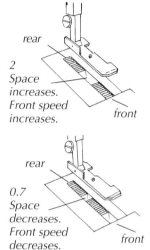

rear

2
Space increases.
Front speed increases.

front

rear

0.7
Space decreases.
Front speed decreases.

front

If the differential feed dial is set below 1 (usually 0.7), the front feed dog takes in a fraction as much fabric under the foot as the rear feed dog releases. The result is the same as "taut sewing," except the machine does the work for you!

NOTE: We've recently found stitch length changes when you turn on differential feed. Keep this in mind if you use it in only part of a garment.

NEEDLES

Consult your manual or dealer to be sure you buy the right needle SYSTEM for your serger. There are MANY different systems for sergers. Some models even call for two different needles in the same machine!

Your serger may call for conventional needles, which have a flat side to ensure correct insertion into the needle hole. If your machine calls for industrial needles, you have probably noticed they are round. Take a close look. On both types you should see (or feel with your fingernail) a long groove which is always on the FRONT side of the needle and a scarf (tiny cutout) which is always on the back side. (Check the side view to see the scarf.) During sewing, the thread lies in the long groove, and the scarf makes room for the looper to come close to the needle to pick up the thread to form a stitch.

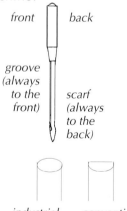

front   back

groove
(always
to the
front)

scarf
(always
to the
back)

industrial   conventional

Whenever you're sewing or serging a knitted fabric that has a tendency to run, use ballpoint needles if possible. If your serger takes conventional machine needles, you should have no trouble finding ballpoint ones to fit. Industrial ballpoint needles are newly available on the market, however, so you may need to search for them.

During our 4-day serger workshops in Portland, Oregon, we've found the most common stitching problem is caused by a bad needle (even a new needle can have an imperfection), or a needle inserted improperly, or not pushed all the way up into the needle slot.

NOT JUST ONE STITCH...OH SO MANY!

To date, sergers can form six basic stitch types. Many machines are convertible and can do several different stitches. Below are the different stitch types with a discussion of the combinations available.

3-thread overlock—The threads connect or "lock at the seam line, and the stitch looks approximately the same on both sides. The stitch is stretchy, so it is ideal for seaming knits. Some machines sew up to a 7 mm stitch width. To make this stitch, the upper looper goes over the top of the fabric leaving a loop which is caught by the needle. The lower looper goes under the fabric placing a loop of thread under the needle loop then goes out to the edge where it knits together with the upper looper thread.

3/4-thread overlock—This is a 3-thread stitch with an extra needle thread running down the middle. You can remove the right needle for a wide 3-thread stitch or remove the left needle for a narrower 3-thread stitch. A 3/4-thread stitch is as stretchy as a 3-thread, so is excellent for knits.

3/4-thread overlock variation—This is a 3-thread stitch with an extra needle, but it looks different from the above 3/4-thread stitch. The lower looper thread is caught by both needles and the upper looper thread by only the right needle leaving a row of what looks like straight stitching next to the serging. This means you MUST use both needles when you want a wide stitch. However, you can leave out the left needle for a narrower stitch. If you leave out the right needle, you will get no stitch at all.

2-thread overedge—Called an "overedge" because the threads do not connect or "lock" at the seam line, so it is not used to sew seams. With only two threads, the stitch produces a lightweight edge finish, better for fine fabrics. (It is also ideal for flatlocking—just sew two layers of fabric with a 2-thread overedge and the seam will pull open—see page 14.) A 2-thread overedge is formed in one of the two ways shown on the next page:

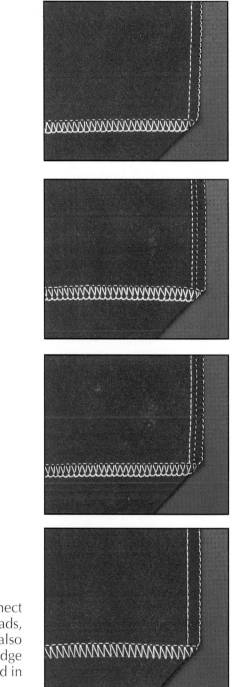

(*2-thread overedge continued*)

THE OVER/UNDER METHOD: The upper looper goes over the top of the fabric leaving a loop of thread that is caught by the needle. Then the upper looper goes under the fabric, picks up the needle thread and pulls it to the edge of the fabric. This method is found on "true" 4-thread machines that do a chain stitch.

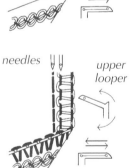

THE PLAY CATCH METHOD: You unthread and plug up the upper looper, turning it into a "V"-shaped "hook." The lower looper goes under the fabric and hands a loop of thread to the upper looper which then places it on top of the fabric ready to be caught by the needle. This method is used on machines that do 3-thread stitches where the upper looper only goes back and forth over the top of the fabric only and cannot go over AND under the fabric.

NOTE: One manufacturer has coined the term "seamlock" for a 2-thread stitch on which the tension has been adjusted so that the threads do not pull apart at the seam line. The "seamlock" calls for the needle tension to be tightened until it forms a straight line and the looper tension to be loosened until it wraps the edge.

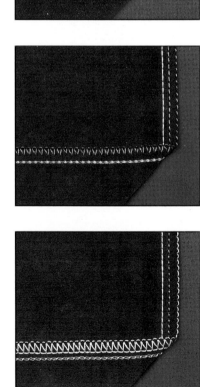

2-thread chain stitch—This stitch, formed by the interaction of the left needle and the lower looper, is found on "true" 4-thread and 5-thread machines. A few machines can also form this chain and sew it anywhere within the fabric, not just next to an edge. It can be used alone or in combination with other stitches.

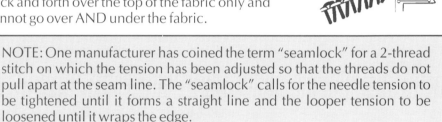

4-thread stitch ("true 4-thread")—A combination of the 2-thread chain and the 2-thread overedge stitch. It is intended for seaming woven fabrics because the edge is finished at the same time the stable chain sews the seam. To sew a seam AND finish the edge, all four threads MUST be used. This makes it different from 3/4-thread machines.

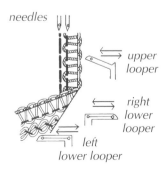

5-thread stitch—Consists of a 2-thread chain stitch and a 3-thread overlock stitch, both described above. Some 5-thread machines can convert the 3-thread overlock stitch to a 2-thread overedge using the "play catch" method described above. All of these stitches can be used alone. We recently heard that one company developed a new throat plate that now allows the machine to sew a 3/4-thread stitch as well. WOW! A machine that "does it all." But, before you run out and buy a 5-thread, remember that you'll have THREE loopers to thread. Decide whether you want one serger that does it all or TWO SERGERS—the ultimate luxury as described in our introduction!

STITCH WIDTH

Stitch width is adjusted either by turning a dial that moves the stitch finger and knives (infinite widths available) or by simply changing the position of a needle to the right or the left needle hole (such machines offer a choice of two widths other than narrow rolled edging).

Some machines have a 7.5 mm stitch width capability with a 3-thread stitch, others a 5mm maximum and some just a 3.5 mm maximum width. If you plan to do a lot of decorative serging, you may prefer a machine that sews at least a 5 mm 3-thread stitch width. Chain stitch machines will generally give you the widest seam, but not necessarily the widest 2- or 3-thread stitch.

This photograph shows the different stitch widths just slightly smaller than actual size.

STITCH LENGTH

Stitch length is adjusted by turning a dial that adjusts the amount of fabric the feed dogs move. Most machines can sew a very short stitch length (0.5 mm) up to a long stitch length (4-5 mm). Sometimes a *slight* change in stitch length will improve the look of your stitch.

This photograph shows 3 mm, 5 mm, and 2 mm stitch lengths slightly smaller than actual size. 2 mm created a "satin" or close stitch with our topstitching thread. Finer threads would require a 0.5-1 mm stitch length to be "satiny."

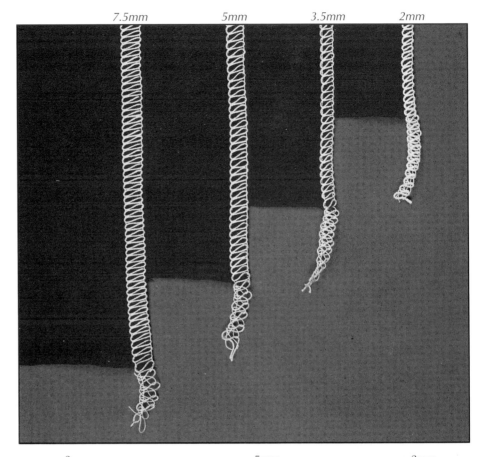

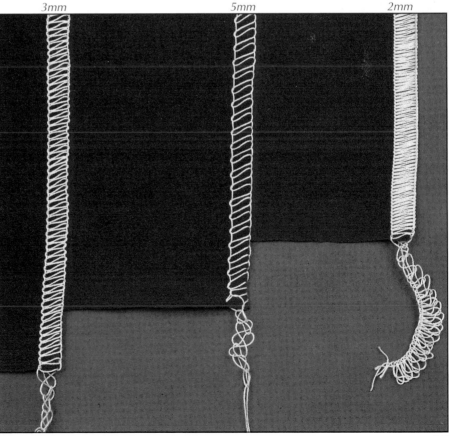

TENSION TIPS

Mastering tension adjustment is the key to enjoying the full capability and versatility of your serger. Think of the tension dials as "pattern adjusters." If you never learn to adjust tension on a serger, you'll be able to do only one stitch. But if you want to flatlock, do rolled hems, or use exciting decorative threads, you'll need to be able to know which way to turn each tension dial. Before you can begin "playing" with tension for decorative effects, you must first learn how to achieve balanced tension. We'll use a 3-thread stitch as our example:

Balanced 3-thread tension:

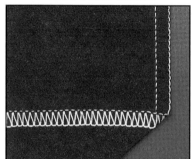

The perfect stitch is one where the upper and lower looper threads meet at the edge and slightly hang off it. You will notice the width of the loops on the top is the same as on the bottom. The upper and lower looper are balanced.

Imbalanced 3-thread tension examples:

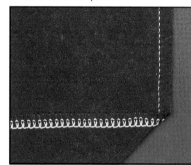

Here, the upper looper thread is pulled to the underside. To balance, always loosen the one that is too tight first. Loosen the lower looper until it comes out to the edge. Serge to check. Then tighten upper looper if necessary.

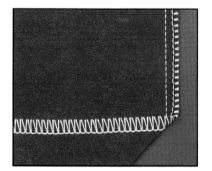

In this case, the lower looper thread is pulled to the top. Loosen the upper looper until it comes out to the edge. Test serge. Check to see if you now need to tighten the lower looper.

Now check the needle

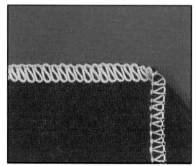

If the needle thread forms loops on the underside, tighten the needle thread tension. (However, with decorative threads, this is sometimes caused by the lower looper being too tight instead—experiment!)

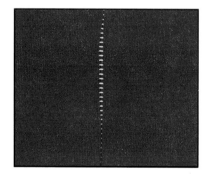

If you pull on your seam and you can see the needle thread, you'll need to tighten the needle tension to have a stronger seam.

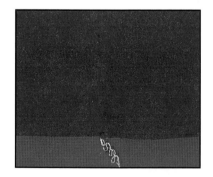

If your seam puckers, it is usually an indication that the needle tension is too tight.

Heavier threads and yarns or ribbons require tension settings different from those for regular serger thread. Heavier threads create more resistance in the tension dials; they simply take up more room. As a result, they call for the tension to be looser.

If your heavy thread is in the upper looper and you have loosened that dial as much as possible only to find the tension is still too tight, try tightening the lower looper to counteract.

If the tension is still a problem, remove the upper looper thread from one or more thread guides, as long as it doesn't adversely affect feeding. As a last resort, remove the thread from the upper looper tension disk itself. EXPERIMENT!

Remove thread from a few guides and tension dial if necessary.

NOTE: If your machine has inset dials, put a piece of Scotch® Brand Magic Transparent Tape over the dial to keep the thread out.

Stitch width affects tension

If you change from a very wide width to a narrow one, less thread is required to form the loops. You would generally need to tighten the looper tensions. If you change from a narrow to a wide stitch, you would need to loosen the tensions to let more thread out of the disks to cover the wider width.

Tape over dials

Stitch length affects tension

If you INCREASE stitch length significantly, you will find your looper threads will tighten up against the edge causing pokeys and sometimes tunneling. More thread is needed to travel the longer distance from stitch to stitch. You need to loosen the tensions of both loopers, letting more thread through, until the loops hang slightly over the edge again.

If you DECREASE stitch length significantly (as shown in center of photo), you will find your looper threads looking sloppy. There is simply too much thread. Less thread is needed for shorter stitch lengths. Tighten the looper tensions, letting less thread through. Sometimes a slight difference in stitch length will improve the look of the stitch.

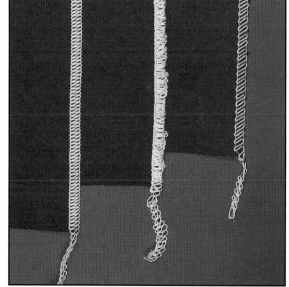

2.5 mm, 1mm, 5 mm with no tension adjustment

Thickness of fabric affects tension

Bulkier fabrics can call for more thread to be released as the distance between the bottom and top has increased. You will often need to loosen tensions. Otherwise, the loopers hug the edge too tightly, and may even cause "tunneling" of the fabric and "pokeys." On the other hand, thinner fabrics and decreased stitch width and length call for tighter than average tensions, or the stitches may be too loopy and look sloppy.

NOTE: For in-depth explanations of EVERYTHING you need to know about tension, see **Sewing with Sergers** by Pati Palmer and Gail Brown, and **Creative Serging** by Pati Palmer, Gail Brown and Sue Green.

FUN WITH FLATLOCKING

Two-Thread Flatlock

When sergers were first introduced to the home-sewing public, the only flatlocking method known was accomplished with a 2-thread overedge stitch. When used to sew a seam, you can pull it open and have a flattened seam similar to stitching seen on ready-to-wear sweatshirts and the like.

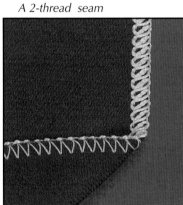

A 2-thread seam

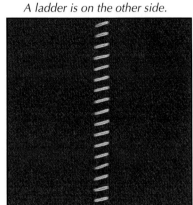

Pull it open to flatten. Loops are on one side.

A ladder is on the other side.

Three-Thread Flatlock

But when most home-sewers came to prefer the versatility of 3-thread or 3/4-thread sergers, Palmer/Pletsch Associates and other experts began experimenting to find a way to sew a 3-thread flatlock. We learned to alter the tension of a 3-thread overlock stitch until it simulated the 2-thread overedge. The result is a stitch that flattens when stress is placed on the two serged layers. Here's how:

1. Loosen the needle tension nearly all the way until the thread forms a "V" on the under side. Then tighten the lower looper until the thread almost disappears and forms a nearly straight line on the edge. Doesn't this now look like a 2-thread overedge? IF YOUR STITCH DOESN'T LOOK LIKE THIS BEFORE YOU FLATTEN THE FABRIC, YOU WILL NOT HAVE A FLATLOCK!

2. Now gently pull the seam open and it will flatten. If one side buckles under the stitches, it isn't flat enough. Loosen the tension on that side (needle tension for the ladder side or the upper looper tension for the loop side).

3. On the top side you will see the loops of the upper looper. You will barely see a straight line on the right edge of the upper looper thread. That is the lower looper thread. On the under side, you will see a "ladder" formed by the needle thread.

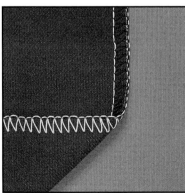

> NOTE: It is sometimes difficult to get the lower looper tight enough for 3-thread flatlocking. Try one of the following:
>
> - **_Use texturized nylon thread in the lower looper._** It affects the tension the same as tightening the tension dial 2 or 3 numbers.
> - **_Wrap your thread around the lower looper tension dial twice._** Loosen the tension, then GRADUALLY tighten while serging SLOWLY so you won't chance bending the lower looper.
> - **_Some sergers have an EXTRA lower looper tension disk for rolled hem._** It can be used for flatlocking as well.

Stitch width and length for flatlocking.

Use the widest stitch when flatlocking. It will be easier to flatten and you'll catch more fabric in the stitch for greater durability. Stitch length is a matter of personal preference. Set it short when the look of a solid band of color is desired. A longer stitch allows the eye to see the fabric through the individual stitches. Experiment to find the best effect for the project at hand.

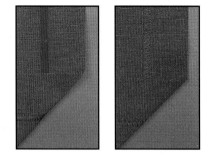

Flatlocking is reversible.

When you desire **_loops on the right side,_** start with WRONG sides of your fabric together. Most of the decorative threads can be used in the upper looper.

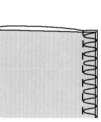

For the **_ladder on the right side,_** start RIGHT sides together. Remember, if you want a decorative thread for the ladder, it must fit through the NEEDLE. Woolly Nylon, lightweight silk and rayon, topstitching thread, and even Decor 6 (a rayon slightly heavier than topstitching thread) all work.

To cut or not to cut? A common question!

When flatlocking **_raw edges_** together, leave the knife engaged to trim off the excess seam allowance as you stitch. This will ensure that the width of the seam is uniform and that you have neat, clean edges.

When flatlocking **_on the fold,_** however, do not cut. In fact, the fabric will flatten better if you let the stitches hang off the edge. We usually don't raise the knife when flatlocking on the fold. It makes us pay attention and we end up serging straighter. But, it's your choice!

Stitches hang off the edge

Stabilize woven fabrics when flatlocking.

Seams in knits can be flatlocked without worry. Wovens, however, may ravel out. Serge a test seam and pull to check strength of the seam. If it ravels, try one of the following:

Serge the edges and press under the seam allowances. Flatlock the folded edges together. (See pages 64-65"fagoting".)

Flatlock the raw edges together and fuse a strip of fusible knit interfacing behind the flattened seam.

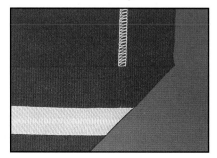

VARIATIONS ON FLATLOCKING

Throughout the book, you will see many variations of flatlocking on the garments photographed. Refer to the index in the back of this book for places where the following flatlocking options appear along with how-to directions.

"Frame" the loops of the flatlock

For a 2-thread flatlock use a contrasting color thread in the needle. For a 3-thread flatlock use a contrasting thread in the NEEDLE **and** LOWER LOOPER of a 3-thread stitch.

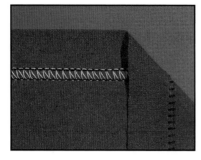

"Float" the loops of the flatlock

Use clear nylon filament thread in the NEEDLE of a 2-thread flatlock or the NEEDLE **and** LOWER LOOPER of a 3-thread stitch. (Or try a lightweight thread that matches the upper looper thread.)

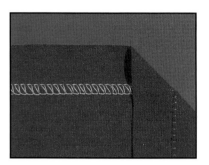

Flatlock over ribbon

Select ribbon which is slightly narrower than the stitch. Fold the fabric, wrong sides together. Place ribbon along fold and flatlock, keeping ribbon inside the stitch.

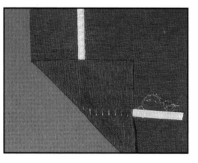

Flatlock fagoting

Create this delicate, hand-crafted look on light- or medium-weight cottons, linens and silks. (See page 65 for how-to details.)

Flatlock shirring

An easy way to shirr a fabric is to flatlock on the wrong side of the fabric over elastic cording. Pull up on the elastic to simulate shirring. (See pages 62-63 for how-to details.)

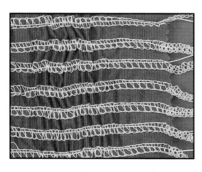

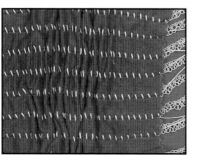

Flatlock fringe

This finish looks great on scarves, shawls, skirt hems, placemats, and napkins. Decorative thread defines the fringe. (See page 147 for how-to details.)

ROLLED EDGE REVIEW

Some people buy a serger just to be able to do a rolled edge! It's a wonderful finish for scarves, table linens, and ruffles. You can match your thread and fabric or do a decorative contrast. Variegated threads are particularly interesting.

variegated Woolly Nylon used on napkins

The "stitch finger"

The rolled edge results from a change in the stitch finger. Some machines allow you to convert to a narrow stitch finger by moving a lever or two, while others require changing the throat plate, on which the stitch finger is located. Some machines also recommend changing the presser foot to facilitate rolling. Consult your manual for instructions for your model.

Because the distance between the knives and the needle does not change when you switch to roll hemming, the fabric rolls around the narrower stitch finger.

knife→

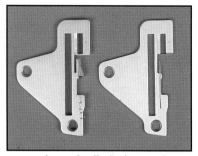

regular and rolled edge stitch

3-Thread Rolled Edge Tension Adjustments

Tighten the lower looper tension nearly all the way. The lower looper thread should form a straight line on the under side of the fabric. As a result, the upper looper thread totally encases the roll. If the upper looper thread isn't wrapping the edge, try loosening the tension. If it isn't forcing the edge to "roll," try tightening the tension.

> NOTE: If you can't get the lower looper thread tight enough, remember what we suggested for flatlocking (see page 19). Try texturized nylon in the lower looper or try wrapping the tension dial twice, but do it at your own risk as it is not recommended in the manuals.

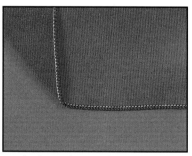

the lower looper thread is green

2-Thread Rolled Edge Tension Adjustments

If your serger can do a 2-thread rolled edge, it is advantageous for lighter-weight fabrics like bridal veil netting and chiffon. In that case, the NEEDLE tension is tightened until the looper thread rolls from the top to the underside and encases the edge.

Rolled Edge Stitch Length

A shorter stitch length is usually used for a rolled edge. However, it is best to start at a 2.0 mm stitch length and gradually shorten until you achieve the look you like. Sometimes too short a stitch length will cause the rolled edge to fall off, especially along the crosswise grain. Check the durability of your test sample. Any stitch length is fine if it gives you the look you want. In fact, a longer stitch length (3-4 mm) is used in ready-made scarves.

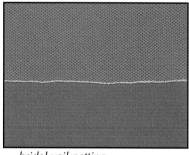

bridal veil netting

stitch length too short

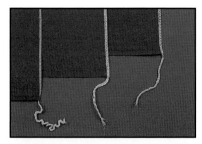

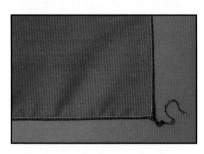

BUT MY ROLLED EDGE ISN'T PERFECT!

Don't worry, we've seen most of the problems during our serger workshops and have come up with solutions.

The stitches do not cover the edge—If your rolled edge thread is a different color than your fabric, you may see your fabric through the stitching (right in photo). Try shortening the stitch length. If that doesn't work, try two strands of thread in the upper looper (center in photo), or use a thread that will cover better, like Woolly Nylon, in the upper looper (left in photo).

Rolled edge puckers—The needle tension may be too tight, the needle may be too large, or the stitch length too short. Also, make sure you are always trimming a little off the edge so the same amount of fabric is always rolling under. On some fabrics, YOU JUST CAN'T ELIMINATE PUCKERS. The crosswise grain on napkins made of a woven poly/cotton fabric will look wonderful, but the lengthwise grain will generally pucker as shown in photo. If you have differential feed, try the .7 setting when you roll the lengthwise edges adjusting stitch length to match crosswise edge if necessary.

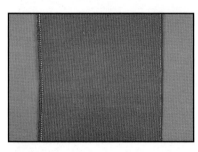

Rolled edge has the "pokeys"—The finished rolled edge will have "whiskers" or little fibers poking out between the stitches. This most often happens with heavier or stiffer woven fabrics. They don't want to roll. Try moving your knives to the right so more fabric rolls under (possible on most machines). Sometimes, a longer stitch length also helps.

Fabric won't roll—For fabrics that resist rolling, move knife over if possible to allow more fabric to roll.

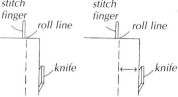

VARIATIONS ON THE ROLLED EDGE

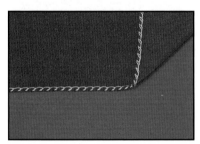

Picot or shell edge—Lengthen the rolled edge stitch to 4 or 5 mm. The upper looper thread will now automatically hug the edge more tightly, causing little scallops or "picots." If the fabric puckers, loosen the needle tension and hold the fabric taut in front of and behind the presser foot while sewing.

Scalloped rolled edge—Serge a rolled edge with the stitch length at 1.5 to 2.0 mm for softness. Then stitch again with a "shell" stitch on a conventional machine. Guide the rolled edge so the "swing" stitch just barely goes over the edge, pulling it in to create a scallop look. Experiment with the blind hem, overlock, and other similar stitches to achieve the effect seen in fine lingerie.

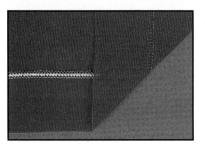

Soutache rolled edge—Set your machine for the rolled edge. Then loosen the needle tension and simply serge on the fold. This creates a design on the fabric that looks like trim or soutache braid. "Frame" the stitch (see flatlocking, page 20) for an interesting look.

Mini blanket stitch—Use the longest stitch length. Loosen the needle thread so that it shows on both sides. Tighten both loopers until both threads lie in a straight line on the edge of the fabric. Limit your thread choices to lightweight ones. You can also get a wider blanket stitch without setting your machine for a rolled edge.

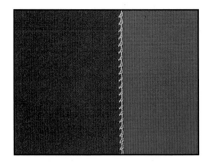

Fish line rolled edge—To add body to the rolled edges of soft fabric ruffles, serge over fish line, encasing the line in the stitch.

1. Cut a strand of fish line (12 to 25 lb.) half again as long as the ruffle strip. Feed line into machine as shown at bottom of page.

2. Using a short, rolled edge stitch, serge over 2 to 3" of the line itself. Then place fabric under presser foot and continue serging. Leave long tail of fishline at end.

3. Stretch edge firmly after serging to spread fabric over fish line. Gather ruffle as usual.

Serger piping—To create soft, custom-color piping, serge over filler cords and strips of bias tricot such as "Seams Great" or "Seam Saver." With the satin rolled edge stitch, serge 2 to 3" over cords, then place tricot strip under foot and continue serging, leaving a 5/8" width of tricot for easy insertion of the piping into a seam. See pages 58, 59, 77 and 103 for more details.

SPECIAL TIPS FOR HANDLING FISHLINE AND OTHER CORDING

If your presser foot has a hole in it for cording, insert the fishline or cord through it and let the machine do the work. If it doesn't, try one of these three options:

Method I

Some presser feet have a lip on the right hand edge. In this case, place your cording to the right of the needle and along the inside of the lip as shown below.

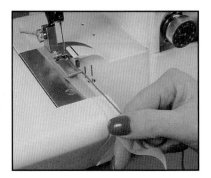

Method II

If there is a space between the sewing bed and the front door or knife cover, place your cording to the right of the needle. Let it fall to the right of the knife between the knife and door as shown below.

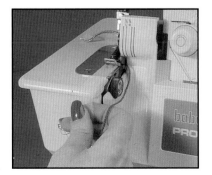

Method III

Place your cording to the right of the needle, over the top left of the upper knife and behind the front door or knife cover as shown below.

THREAD GLOSSARY

Just as sergers keep improving, so does the selection of suitable threads. Not wanting to miss out on this newest trend in the sewing industry, the thread companies are continually developing new threads or experimenting with existing ones, testing their adaptability to the serger.

We find interesting new possibilities most often in yarn stores. Look there for "accompanying yarns for knitting." Many of them work in the serger for unusual textural effects not possible with more conventional threads.

An updated list of thread choices follows, but it is by no means complete. There may very well be other options that we don't yet know about. The following are the most readily available at this time.

Regular Thread—Available in several weights from extra fine to all-purpose. It is used mostly for seaming, edge finishing and roll hemming.

Clear Nylon Monofilament Thread—We generally limit use of this thread to decorative applications where we need one or more of the threads to be "invisible" as in a floating flatlock, flatlocking over ribbon or flatlock fagoting.

> NOTE: An extra-fine semi-transparent polyester thread, such as Metrolene by Wrights/Swiss-Metrosene, may serve the same purpose. It is nearly invisible like clear nylon and is available in 10 colors.

Topstitching Thread—These polyester or cotton-wrapped polyester threads are tightly twisted and just a little heavier than regular thread, so easy to use in both loopers AND the needle. Use a spool cap because the wide angle created by the spool cap helps the parallel wound thread flow more freely. Be sure to place the spool notched end down.

Plan ahead too, since each spool is only 50 yards. (Note: Wrights/Swiss-Metrosene offers 328-yard spools of topstitching thread, but only in a few best-selling colors. Their full color range is available on 55-yard spools.)

"Woolly" texturized nylon

nylon monofilament

transparent Metrolene

Pearl cotton #5

Crochet thread

Metropearl

fine metallic threads

nylon monofilament

Packaged metallic yarn

Pearl cotton #8

Rayon Thread—A number of decorative threads are made of rayon, so when we refer to "fine rayon thread" in this book, we mean fine rayon machine embroidery thread. Its primary characteristic is its beautiful sheen. Familiar brands include Iris, Natesh, Madeira, and Sulky.

"Decor 6" is a medium-weight, untwisted rayon cord available to stores and consumers through Palmer/Pletsch. Originally offered as an accompanying yarn for knitting, it "fills in" more than regular thread to make a bolder statement. Its lack of twist gives it exceptional luster, but also makes it more fragile than twisted threads. For this reason, we recommend it (and other untwisted threads) for better clothing that will receive TLC. We have used it in both loopers as well as in the needle (for flatlocking). "Metropearl" is a new twisted rayon cord made specifically for serger sewing from Wrights/Swiss-Metrosene. It can also be used in both loopers.

Cotton Embroidery Floss has the sheen of silk and rayon threads, but just enough difference in texture to yield yet another look. If in a skein, "unwrap" it into one long "rope" before threading it into the machine, and keep an eye on it during use to be sure it doesn't tangle. Madeira sells it on a reel.

Silk Thread—Harder to find and more costly than rayon, we mention it because the topstitching weight (silk buttonhole twist) lends a touch of luxury.

Texturized Nylon—YLI introduced the original "Woolly Nylon," and now several companies manufacture texturized nylon, with a crimped, fuzzy quality resembling wool. This thread can be used in the needle as well as the loopers. It's extra strong yet soft and comfortable next to the skin, making it perfect for swimwear. Use a press cloth, as a hot iron can melt the thread. Avoid chlorine bleach which can cause yellowing of whites.

Acrylic Thread—Lightweight acrylic threads, such as those for punch needle embroidery, yield a yarn-like quality without the bulk. Look in yarn craft stores for names such as Pretty Punch. Burmilana (70% acrylic and 30% wool) is available in a heavier weight with or without a metallic thread loosely twisted around it to combine the matte quality of yarn with a bit of shine.

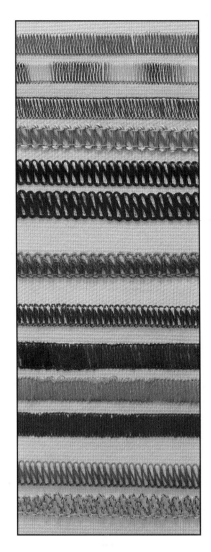

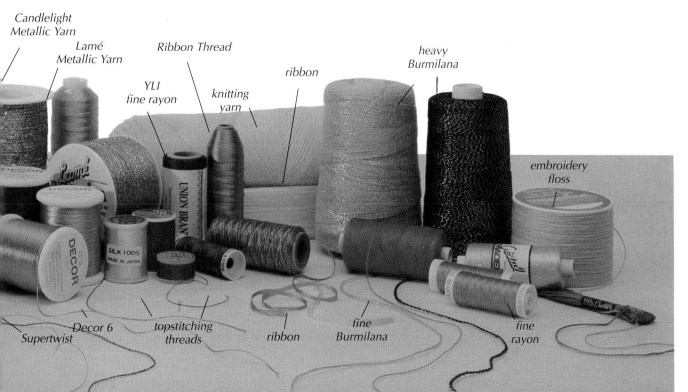

Candlelight Metallic Yarn

Lamé Metallic Yarn

Ribbon Thread

heavy Burmilana

ribbon

YLI fine rayon

knitting yarn

embroidery floss

Supertwist

Decor 6

topstitching threads

ribbon

fine Burmilana

fine rayon

Metallic Thread—Great for evening and bridal apparel and costumes. Test for differences among brands. Some are very fine, resembling silk, while others are coarse and metal-like. Some will strip back and fray when used in the needle and lower looper, so we recommend using them in the upper looper only.

"Supertwist" is the brand name of Madeira's very fine metallic embroidery thread of 70% nylon and 30% metalized polyester. We use it in the serger as an "accompanying thread"—always in combination with another thread in the same looper—just to give shine and textural interest.

Metallic yarn, a blend of rayon, polyester, and metal, has the same qualities as the finer threads; it's just bulkier. For this reason, it is a little trickier to use; but it imparts a bolder, more defined edge to medium and heavyweight fabrics. Brand names include Candlelight by YLI and Lamé by Madeira.

Madeira offers another version labeled "metallic effect yarn for knitting and embroidery," which is 60% metal and 40% polyester. It's similar in weight to the Lamé, but less twisted for a smoother shine. Oddly, it comes looped in a package, but simply punch a hole in the package and put the whole thing on the spool pin. The yarn unreels without tangling (see photo page 67). With only 22 yards to a package, it compels you to plan ahead!

Crochet Thread—Available in many colors in cotton or acrylic, this tightly-twisted cord is slightly thicker than topstitching thread. The acrylic variety is fuzzier than the cotton, making it an ideal coordinate for wools and sweater knits. Knit Crosheen by Coats & Clark is easily found.

Pearl Cotton—This all-cotton cord is similar to crochet thread, but its looser twist gives it a soft, pretty sheen as well. Two weights are appropriate for serger sewing—#8 (finer) and #5 (thicker).

Available in a broad range of colors plus variegated shades, pearl cotton #5 can be found in 10-yard skeins or 50-yard balls, while #8 comes on 95-yard balls from DMC. In addition, Coats & Clark now offers 150-yard cones of pearl cotton #5 with a special finish applied to the thread to make it easier to use in the serger.

Ribbon—Generally, stick with soft knitting ribbons 1/16 to 1/8" wide and use them just in the upper looper. Most polyester ribbons that you find on rolls in fabric stores have thick selvages that make them too stiff for use in the serger. Ribbon creates an unusual, braid-like edge because it "stands" on edge.

Another new product for decorative serging is Ribbon Thread by Metier de Geneve. Available on 100-meter spools, it sews like thread, but looks like ribbon. The color selection covers the spectrum, including several metallics and a wider (1/4") ribbon in a choice of multi-metallics or opalescent white. While regular Ribbon Thread is all rayon, the metallics are a blend of 55% polyester and 45% nylon. Ribbon Floss, a similar product by Rhode Island Elastic Co., is less expensive, but comes on 40-yard spools in only 15 colors.

Yarn—Limit your choices to those that are fine, strong, tightly twisted and smooth. Pull on a strand. If it breaks easily, it will also break easily when serging. If too loosely twisted, it can be caught by the needle and jam your machine. If too hairy or lumpy (with slubs), it won't flow evenly through the tension and thread guides. Machine knitting yarns work well.

Use yarn in the upper looper only. Check the weight by running two strands through the looper eye. If you can't force a double strand through, then you can assume that one strand will not feed easily enough to work successfully.

If your machine fights even the finer yarns, you're not alone! Give up rather than damage your serger.

DECORATIVE THREAD TIPS

Use the decorative thread where it will show.

Generally, a decorative thread is used in the upper looper because that is the thread that shows; it's the one on "top." Fewer threads work successfully in the lower looper because the additional thread guides add more stress.

Make a "thread cradle."

Threading heavy and/or untwisted threads through the loopers is easy with a dental floss threader, available in most drug stores. You can also use a strand of regular thread to form a thread "cradle." Wrap it around the heavier thread forming a loop. Then thread BOTH ends of the regular thread through the looper eye, pulling the heavier thread through with it. This also works for texturized nylon and other hard-to-thread threads.

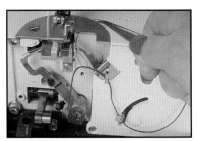

dental floss threader

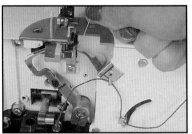

thread cradle

"Clear" your threads.

"Clear" threads before beginning to stitch by bringing all threads up. Use a pin to pull up needle thread. This prevents the needle thread from looping around loopers.

Then put all threads under presser foot. The foot will hold the threads in place while you form your chain.

use a pin to clear

pull up needle thread

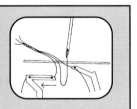

put all threads under presser

Then rotate the handwheel by HAND to see if the stitches are forming a chain on the stitch finger.

NOTE: If you reverse flywheel, which moves lower looper to left, the needle thread "loop" will slip off the lower looper. This will help you pull out unchained threads when needed (see index).

The "bridge"

When using heavier threads, the chain needs to be under the "bridge" of the presser foot when you begin to serge.

Make sure threads are "engaged."

Check that threads are engaged in tension disks by tugging on them just above and below the dials. You should feel resistance on each thread.

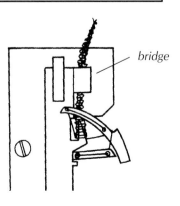

bridge

Spool caps.

When using parallel-wound spools, always place the notch down and use the spool caps that come with the machine. The wide angle created by the cap helps the thread reel off the top freely and evenly. Check your manual for correct placement of the caps. Sometimes they are inserted on the spools themselves which are then placed on the spool rods; on other models the caps are simply placed atop the spool rods.

Thread Nets

If the thread is very slippery, such as rayon, nylon and many metallics, cover the spool with serger thread nets to prevent spilling or slipping off the bottom of the spool. After placing the net on the spool, fold it back on itself to allow the thread to flow smoothly without resistance and hiccups. Try nylon thread nets, available from your serger dealer, finger and toe gauze, or pantyhose seamed into small tubes.

Hiccups

Any restriction on your thread will cause a "hiccup"—as if you suddenly increased the tension. Hiccups happen when thread catches on something, such as nylon nets or the notch on a spool, or when thread doesn't reel freely off the spool, ball or skein.

Snaking Thread

If your thread, yarn or ribbon is not wound on spools or cones, you must start with a loose "pool" of thread to feed freely into the serger. Place the ball or skein on the table behind the machine, then reel off a large quantity and serge—reel and serge—reel and serge and so on. It looks like a long "snake." Any restriction on the thread will cause uneven stitching, so be sure there's always plenty of slack between the ball or skein and the first thread guide.

Rewinding thread

You can also rewind thread from balls or skeins onto an empty (or full) cone or spool. If hand winding, "crosswind" by moving the spool back and forth as you wind.

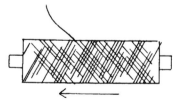

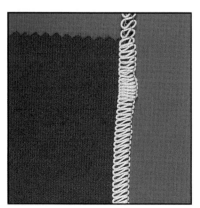

Lift the presser foot.

It is often not necessary to lift the presser foot for regular serging, but you MUST LIFT the foot and place the fabric under it when using decorative threads. It helps prevent **stacking of the stitches**, as shown in the photo, so "feeding" begins smoothly. You may also need to gently tug on the chain when beginning to serge.

Begin sewing SLOWLY!

We can't emphasize this enough. Although your serger was made for speed, heavier threads pose a variety of potential problems. In addition, serging too fast can place extra tension on the thread resulting in uneven stitching. Check your stitches every few inches.

Skim the edge.

Always at least skim the fabric edge with the knives to neaten the edge and to help maintain an even stitch width (unless serging on a fold!).

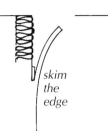

skim the edge

or stitches may not hug the edge

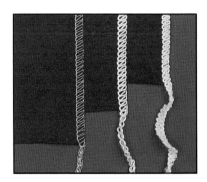

Begin with a long stitch length.

The bulkiness of the thread affects stitch length. We strongly recommend increasing stitch length to 3.5 mm when working with heavy threads, to prevent jamming under the presser foot. You can then gradually shortening the stitch length until the desired look is achieved.

In the photo, all threads were serged with a 3 mm stitch length. Notice how the heavier threads fill up the spaces.

ALWAYS TEST FIRST!

It's difficult—and time-consuming—to correct a mistake, so testing is essential to successful serging.

Test with a L-O-N-G strip of fabric.

To save time, use LONG strips of fabric rather than several short ones. That way, you can serge a couple inches, check the stitch top **and** underside, make any changes in settings, serge another couple inches, and so on. It's faster than always taking the fabric out of the machine and starting over. Depending on your model, you may be able to change tensions, stitch length AND width without ever taking the fabric out of the machine.

In addition, using one long strip gives you a "record" of the changes you made, and it will be easier to choose the look you like best. Otherwise, your "trials" end up in the serger waste-catcher!

Test on garment fabric.

Always test-serge on scraps of the same fabric as the actual garment, through the same number of layers, and on the same grain. Serging may respond differently, for example, on the bias than on the straight grain.

Check tension every 6" on test sample.

Adjust only ONE TENSION DIAL AT A TIME so you can see the results of the change you just made! Always loosen the thread tension that is too tight first. When you are satisfied with the look of the stitch for the project at hand, it's time to SERGE AHEAD!

Buy the right amount of thread.

As a rule, allow approximately seven yards of thread per looper for every one yard of decorative serging. In other words, if the special thread will be in both loopers, plan on 14 yards per yard of serging— more for very thin threads. Add about 10 yards for testing. These allowances are based on a serger stitch length of 2.5 mm and a width of 5 mm. Of course, if you change the length and width, the yardage you'll need will vary.

a test strip

DECORATIVE THREAD CHART

	Thread Type	Fiber Content	Needle(s)	Needle Size
SILKIES	Fine silk	Silk	Yes	12/80 or smaller
	Fine rayon	Rayon	Yes	12/80 or smaller
	Decor 6	Rayon (untwisted)	Yes	14/90
	Embroidery floss	Cotton	Too thick	N/A
METALLICS	Fine metallic	Rayon/metallized polyester	Yes	12/80
	Madeira's Supertwist	Nylon/polyester	Yes	12/80
	Metallic yarn, e.g., Candlelight Lamé	Rayon/metalized polyester	Too thick	N/A
BULKIES	Topstitching thread	Cotton-covered polyester, polyester or silk	Yes	14/90
	Texturized nylon, e.g., Wooly Nylon, Metroflock, Bulky Lock	Nylon	Yes	12/80 or smaller
	Crochet thread, e.g., Knit-Cro-Sheen	Cotton or acrylic	Too thick	N/A
	Pearl cotton	Cotton	Too thick	N/A
	Mettler's Metropearl	Rayon	Too thick	N/A
	Madeira's Burmi-lana #12	Wool/acrylic	No (hiccups)	N/A
	Madeira's Burmi-lana #3	Wool/acrylic/metallic	Too thick	N/A
	Yarn	Any	Too thick	N/A
RIBBONS	Soft ribbon	Silk, polyester, rayon or acrylic	Too thick	N/A
	Ribbon Thread™ Ribbon Floss	Rayon	Too thick	N/A
CLEAR	Nylon Monofilament	Nylon	Yes	12/80

Upper Looper	Lower Looper	Tension	Minimum Stitch Length
Yes	Yes	Slightly tighter	Shortest
Yes	Can break	Slightly tighter	Shortest
Yes	Sometimes tends to skip	Looser	2.0
Yes	Too thick	Looser	2.0
Yes	May fray	Normal	Shortest
Yes	Yes	Normal	Shortest
Yes	Sometimes	Looser	2.0
Yes	Yes	Looser	1.0
Yes	Yes	Looser	Shortest
Yes	Okay	Looser	2.0
Yes	Too thick	Looser	2.0
Yes	Yes	Looser	1.5
Yes	Yes	Looser	1.0
Yes	Too thick	Looser	2.0
Yes	Too thick	Looser	2.0 or longer
Yes	Too thick	Looser	2.0
Yes	Yes	Looser	2.0
Yes	Yes	Normal	Shortest

The Extraordinary

Couching on a Serger

You can create your own designer fabric on a serger using the decorative "couching" technique of applying cords or yarns to the surface of a fabric by sewing over them. It is a technique we never even mentioned in our first two books on serger sewing, but it has been done to striking effect in this black cocoon jacket made by Lynn Raasch, the "Kissy Fish" sweatshirt created for McCall's by Pati Palmer and Susan Pletsch, and the jersey dress by Marta Alto. The serger was used for every stitch, from couching the fuzzy, nubby yarn onto the fabrics to actually sewing the pieces together.

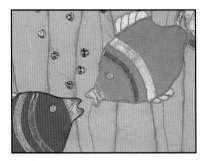

The yarn has been flatlocked in place using clear nylon thread. The only thread showing on the right side of the fabric is the inconspicuous "ladder" of the needle.

Use a pattern with few seams so there will be fewer places to match the yarn "stripes." Lynn felt it important to match the front seams on her cocoon jacket. However, Pati felt it more interesting to leave the sweatshirt shoulder seams unmatched.

1. Cut out garment.

2. Place yarn on right side of fabric, planning for yarn stripes on front and back to come together at seam lines, as necessary. Tape at intervals with Scotch® Brand Magic Tape to hold yarn in place.

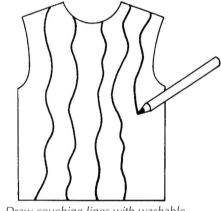

Draw couching lines with washable marker, matching seams if desired.

3. Machine baste yarn to fabric. This will hold yarn in place and gives you a line to follow when you flatlock from the wrong side.

4. Fold right sides together on couching (basting) lines. (You may find it helpful to press the folds.)

5. Using clear nylon thread in the needle and regular thread in the loopers, flatlock on the fold with your longest stitch length, catching yarn in the process. Open the fabric and VOILÀ—The yarn appears to be "floating" on the surface!

Machine baste yarn to fabric (left). Flatlock with yarn folded to inside, using nylon thread

You could also do this technique by flatlocking from the right side with flatlock LOOPS over the yarn. Fold fabric wrong sides together and lengthen the stitch to 5. Put clear nylon thread in the upper looper. The advantage of this method is that you don't have to baste to be sure the yarn stays in place—you can see it as you serge. The disadvantage is that the loops may show more than the ladders in the method above.

Marta Alto created her beautiful black cocoon jacket from a wool jersey and added appliqués of Ultrasuede Facile and silky prints. She serged the outside edge of each with a metallic thread in the upper looper, then topstitched the appliqués on conventionally.

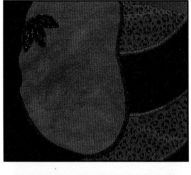

Marta used similar methods when she combined silky polyester charmeuse with Ultrasuede Facile appliqués and random flatlocking to create a striking interplay of colors, textures, and freeform shapes. The single row of flatlocking with black Candlelight metallic yarn across the front, over the shoulders and down the back of the sleeve, gives the impression that all the rows of black are flatlocking. Not so!

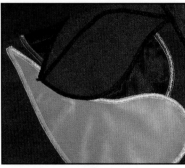

How can you duplicate this look yourself?

1. Sew the shoulder seams of the top first so the appliqués and flatlocking can go from front to back OVER the shoulder.

2. Back fabric for appliqués with a fusible knit interfacing. Do not use fusible web, as it makes the large areas of satin stiff looking.

3. Cut out appliqué shapes.

4. Serge all edges using different decorative threads on each piece.

5. Steam baste 1/4" strips of fusible web to wrong side of appliqué edges, holding iron 2" above web.

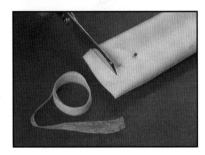

QUICK TIP: Make your own strips—buy a yard of fusible web, fold eight or more times and cut 1/4" strips through all thicknesses.

6. Place appliqués on fabric, lapping as desired. Fuse in place.

7. Topstitch around each appliqué, catching outside edge of serging loops. Change top-stitching thread color to match serging thread.

topstitch

8. Plan placement of flatlock topstitching so that it appears to be a continuation of the serging around one of the appliqués. Mark with chalk or washable marker. Fold on the line and flatlock along the fold from the right side, starting at the back sleeve edge and serging to the appliqué.

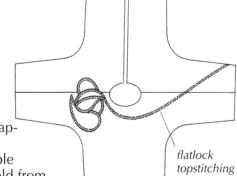

flatlock topstitching

Pull slack, then chain off

SPECIAL TIP: To stop exactly at the appliqué, release stitches from the stitch finger and pull out unchained threads. Move the fabric out from under the presser foot, and chain off.

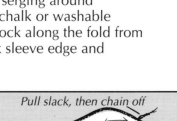

Edging a Cape to Make an Entrance

Couture, Elegant, Lush, Rich—All are descriptions of what Kathleen Spike was wanting to achieve in fashioning her wool cape. Tone-on-tone color mixes create the most sophisticated looks, as is exemplified by the choice of champagne Ribbon Thread for edging. Plus, the textural contrast between the matte wool flannel and the ribbon's subtle sheen exudes luxury.

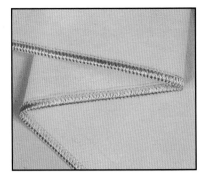

Kathy used ribbon thread in both loopers with texturized nylon in the needle. She found the differential feed set on 2 helped to prevent rippling when serging on the curves (bias grain).

Kathy's cape is easy to make without a pattern! Allow 2 5/8 yards of 60" fabric to make a cape with a finished length of 45"—perfect for someone 5'5" tall who likes a full-length style.

1. Cut yardage in half crosswise. Cut one section in half again, lengthwise. These two "quarters" become the fronts, and the other "half" becomes the back.

2. Join front sections to the back at shoulder seams. (Since capes tend to shift during wear, seams help define the shoulder.)

> NOTE: If cape feels too floppy, try sewing shoulder seams at an angle. This reduces the amount of fabric that falls from the shoulder onto the hip.

3. Scoop out the neckline, then try on to check fit. Kathy recommends the neckline be 5/8" larger that your neck. You may also round all corners of the cape for an edge that is easier to decoratively serge.

4. Add an optional hood. Kathy designed her own pattern, sewing and fitting a muslin until she was happy with the look. After cutting hood from fashion fabric, decoratively serge its center back seam. Serge hood to neckline then serge ties and edge of hood.

> NOTE: If you do not add a hood, you may choose to add a neckline "sweep." Cut a bias strip of fashion fabric 36" to 45" long. Decoratively serge edges. Topstitch to neckline.

5. Decoratively serge all remaining edges. Kathy turned under 5/8" on long straight edges and serged on fold for more body and durability. She also used differential feed set at 2 on curves to prevent stretch. She lengthened the stitch slightly at that time so stitch length would look the same as on the straight edges.

6. Attach closures at neckline (frogs, snaps, buttons or hook-and-loop fastener tape). Kathy used a slide-style belt buckle on the ties of her hood.

❧

Under Kathy's cape, our model wears Pati's pant and top of wool double knit. While its decorative serging may look identical to that on the cape, Pati chose Decor 6 thread instead of Ribbon Thread. Both are shiny for textural interest against the matte fabric, but Ribbon Thread's braided edges help it "stand up" to add more dimension. Decor 6 slips through the loopers more easily, though, so perhaps more sergers could handle it successfully.

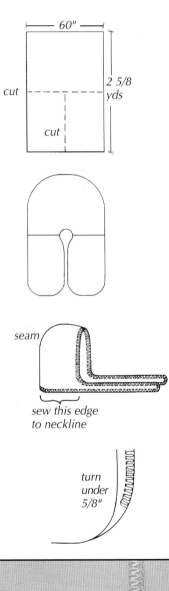

60"

cut

2 5/8 yds

cut

seam

sew this edge to neckline

turn under 5/8"

Suiting with Facile

Because Marta teaches our Ultrasuede® seminars and serger workshops, she wanted to combine the two concepts and make a wool jacket bound with Ultrasuede® Facile® to wear with an Facile skirt. Here's how:

1. Serge-finish seams, facing, and hem allowances of the unlined jacket using Decor 6 in the upper looper. Plan direction of stitching so Decor thread will show when seams are pressed open and hem pressed up.

2. Straight stitch facing to jacket WRONG SIDES TOGETHER on seam line.

3. Trim off entire seam allowance very close to stitching.

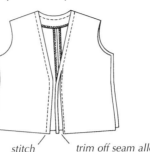

stitch　　　*trim off seam allowance*

4. Cut crosswise strips of Facile 1-1/2" wide and the length of the neckline and fronts of jacket plus a little extra for good measure. Where Facile must be joined, simply lap one edge over the other slightly and stitch. You may want to plan the seam at center back and make the nap run in the same direction on both sides of front.

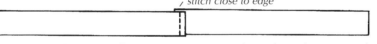

stitch close to edge

5. With Decor 6 in the upper looper, serge one edge of Facile, napped side up, without trimming.

6. Lay serged edge of Facile along jacket front 1/2" from edge, stretching around curve of neckline so it will lie flat; pin.

7. Fold other edge of Facile to under side and repin.

8. Edgestitch through all layers catching loops of Decor 6.

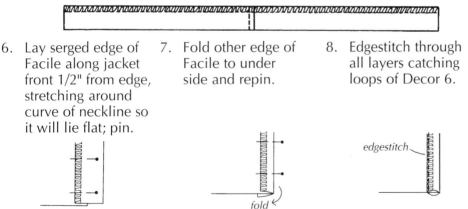

edgestitch

fold

9. Using appliqué scissors, trim away surplus Facile very close to stitching on under side.

❧

Marta's blouse also has a touch of serging on it. Rather than straight stitch along the line that forms the hidden placket, Marta CHAIN-stitched with the same silver Decor 6 thread in the looper. Because the chain forms under the fabric, decorative chain stitching must be done with right side down against the throat plate.

NOTE: As of this writing, the White serger model 216 is the only one that can accommodate a thread as heavy as Decor in the chain looper.

For instructions for making the flower, see accessories page 145.

Creative Tops With glitter

"Glamour-in-a-Day" Wardrobe

The winter white wool doubleknit is perfect for Pati Palmer's totally serged jacket. Eliminate all facings if your fabric has enough body. The challenge...the right **and** wrong side of the fabric AND serging show. This makes for some interesting options. You could use different colored thread in the upper and lower loopers. You could cut a double front out of contrasting fabrics. Pati used light blue metallic ribbon thread in both upper and lower loopers with a 5 mm stitch width and a 4 mm stitch length. The looper tensions were set at 0, but she was able to leave the thread in the tension disks.

SPECIAL TIP: Sewing order is important since you never want to stitch over decorative stitching:

1. Sew center back and shoulder seams.
2. Serge lower edge of sleeve with decorative thread.
3. Sew one underarm and side seam.
4. Decoratively serge outside edges.
5. Sew other underarm and side seam.

SPECIAL TIP: It's easier to serge curves than points. Pati rounded the front of this jacket before serging.

Serger Patchwork With an Artistic Touch

A sweatshirt with sparkle and shine for evening wear! That's what Lynn created when she put metallic fabrics and threads together in a design of Seminole quilting to embellish this ready-to-wear sweatshirt.

Before cutting any strips or squares, Lynn backed the metallic fabrics with fusible knit interfacing to give them more stability for serging. She backed the other fabrics as well, but not by fusing. She just used a cotton batiste and treated the two layers as one.

To duplicate Lynn's design using five different fabrics, do the following:

1. Cut five strips of EACH fabric (25 in total), each 1 1/2" wide and 7 1/2" long.

2. Start with five strips—one of each color. Set other strips aside. With fine metallic thread in the upper looper, serge strips together lengthwise, wrong sides together (seams on the outside). Press all seams in same direction. Lynn used a 3/4-thread stitch for strength with peach and aqua threads in the needles.

3. Take another five strips (one of each color again), alternate the order of the colors, and repeat step 2.

4. Repeat three more times, alternating colors each time so that each of the five stacks of strips is in a different order (see A–E at right).

5. Cut each block into 1 1/2" strips across the seams. Set aside.

6. Arrange strips in desired pattern. Serge together (seams on the outside) to form patchwork.

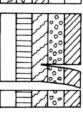

serge fabric into five squares, then cut each into 1 1/2" strips.

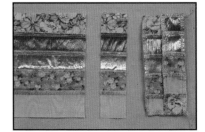

Creative Casual Tops

Rolled Edge Collars

The sporty top with red accent stitching was one of Karen Dillon's first serger projects, and she says she learned a lot while making it! Her main lesson was to do her testing on the same grain as the garment. She used regular thread for the front inset and shoulder seams, but had to switch to texturized nylon for the rounded edges of the collar for better coverage.

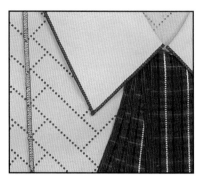

A balanced 3-thread stitch was used to join the shoulder and front inset seams. Karen attached the interfaced under collar to the upper collar wrong sides together, and edged the unit with roll hemming, trimming away the entire seam allowance in the process. It's a quick and easy way to sew collars and cuffs without trimming, turning or edgestitching.

Creative Serging to Match Accessories

Generally, accessorizing comes after the outfit is chosen, but when Ann Price's mother gave her the colorful striped sash, Ann decided to make this top using variegated topstitching thread called "Jeans Thread" from YLI. The colors coordinated perfectly with the sash!

She selected a pattern with an interesting neckline and yoke seam. Flatlocking was an obvious option for the yoke seam, but the crisp cotton would have required special treatment to prevent raveling (see **Creative Serging** p. 53, 54). Instead, Ann did lapped seaming. Here's how:

1. Apply neckline facing, turn and press. Serge along **finished** edge without trimming, using decorative thread in upper looper. Use regular thread in a contrast color in the needle and lower looper in order to "frame" the stitch. By serging the **finished** neckline without cutting, she got an even curve without pokeys.

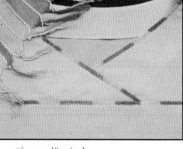

"framed" stitch

2. Finish the raw edges on bottom of yoke and top of bodice using regular serging thread.

regular thread

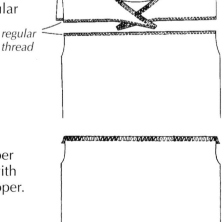

3. To avoid pokeys, press under the upper seam allowance on the upper bodice and serge along the fold with decorative thread in the upper looper. (Serge edge of seam allowance if necessary to prevent raveling.)

4. Lap upper bodice pieces at center front. Lap lower bodice to the seam line of the upper bodice. (Use a strip of fusible web to steam-baste the two together, if desired.) Topstitch at the upper edge of the serging, where straight stitches will be "buried" in the loops.

fusible web

NOTE: Ann chose to lap lower over upper to avoid decorative serging over the lump formed where the yoke laps. On other styles, you may prefer the look of lapping upper over lower bodice.

Faux Golf Cardigan for Men

Pati Palmer and Susan Pletsch designed a Custom Sweatshirt pattern for McCalls. One of the designs (shown to left) inspired Kathy to do a second version (photo on page 42).

Her father-in-law had never worn a sweatshirt, so Kathy decided this "faux"-cardigan style would be a good compromise between an overly casual, basic sweatshirt and the upscale good looks of a cardigan golf sweater. She searched for the best quality fleece and the ribbings that would shape this garment into something special for a special someone. Kathy says it was like putting together the pieces of a puzzle.

Here are the steps used in the McCalls pattern (Kathy varied from these a bit).

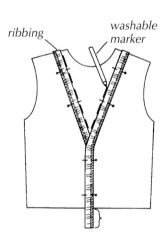
ribbing   *washable marker*

1. Finish unfinished edge of 1 1/2" ribbing by serging with a short wide satin stitch and heavier decorative thread such as pearl cotton #5.

2. Pin single layer ribbing to front to check placement with ribbing extending about 4" below lower edge. It should look like a cardigan sweater. Mark the "V" with chalk or a water soluble marker.

3. Cut a "V" of contrast fabric slightly larger than the "V" formed by the ribbing. Edgestitch to front. (You may cut away excess fabric under the "V" to eliminate bulk or shadow-through.

4. Edge stitch ribbing to front lapping left over right. (Lap right over left if doing this for a woman.) Stop stitching 2" from lower edge of front.

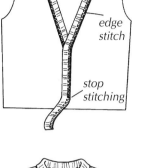

> NOTE: For specific information on applying ribbing, see page 51.

5. Finish sweatshirt.

> NOTE: If using Johnny collar, the **finished** width of the neckline ribbing should not be wider than 5/8".

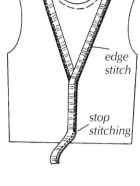

6. Top-stitch remainder of ribbing in place at bottom, turning under lower edge. Hand catch ribbing to wrong side of lower band.

7. Sew on buttons.

JOHNNY COLLARS

These are very popular additions to sweatshirts. Knit collars are available in packages in both adults and children's sizes in the notions department or in stores specializing in knits.

1. Mark center front and back of neck ribbing with pins.

2. Fold knit collar in half. Mark center back with pin.

3. Pin collar to neck edge, matching center backs. Pin front ends of collar 1/2" from center front. This leaves a fashionable amount of ribbing showing at center front.

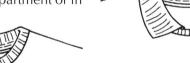

4. Stretch collar to fit neck edge if necessary as you sew.

> NOTE: It may be easier to sew collar conventionally, then serge-finish seam.

5. Press seam allowances toward garment.

Creative Blouses

Flatlock "Ladders" Decorate a Blouse

Lynn designed the criss-cross pattern of stitching to accent this simple top because she wanted to repeat the coarse basket weave of her jacket (see pages 120 and 123). The sleeves are flatlock hemmed to unify the look.

Because the jacket features decorative serging on the inside, Lynn chose the same specialty thread for the flatlocking on her blouse. Since she wanted the "ladders" out, Decor 6 rayon was used in the needle (size 12/80). Matching regular serger thread was used both loopers.

Lynn cut out the pattern then flatlocked the front as follows before putting the pieces together:

1. Mark placement lines on wrong side with vanishing ink marker (test removability on fabric first).

2. Fold on the **horizontal lines**, right sides together, and flatlock on the fold with stitches hanging over the edge. Open flatlocking.

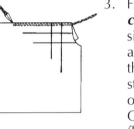

3. Fold on the **vertical lines**, right sides together, and flatlock on the fold with stitches hanging over the edge. Open the flatlocking.

NOTE: When starting and stopping within the fabric, not on an edge, release stitches from stitch finger (see page 115). This allows you to get the fabric under the needle. Stitch to end of placement line, release stitches from finger again, remove fabric, then chain off.

---

4. DO NOT TIE KNOT IN OR USE SEAM SEALANT ON TAIL CHAIN as either may show through fine fabric. You can secure the ends by threading through a blunt pointed tapestry needle and weaving them under the looper threads then back through them in the other direction.

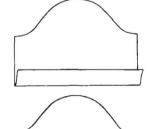

5. Hem the sleeves by flatlocking before they are set into the blouse. Fold hem allowance to the inside, then fold hem width to the outside.

6. With hem allowance against throat plate, flatlock the three layers close to the fold, being careful not to cut it.

7. Pull the hem down until the stitching is flat.

8. Sew blouse together. VOILÀ! A sophisticated touch. Does this inspire you to try it using other fabrics and threads?

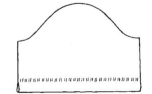

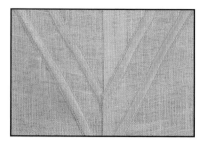

Flatlock "Loops" Decorate A Blouse

An illustration in **Creative Serging** (p. 24) inspired Marta to make this blouse with decorative flatlock topstitching. She soon learned it was not as simple as it had appeared!

For example, if you start flatlocking at the armhole of the sleeve and continue on the diagonal, you will end at the cuff in the back! You can't turn a corner in the middle of the sleeve, so the only way to create a chevron there is to add a seam down the center.

Watch stitching direction when serging parallel rows or rows on opposite sides of a center line. Because one side of a flatlock stitch has a more defined edge than the other (almost a ridge) you will want that edge to be symmetrical from one side of the garment to the other. To accomplish that you need to stitch **down** to the center front, then **up** the other side. Test to see if you see a difference in the look of the stitches.

Getting the rows to chevron perfectly at the center front of the blouse and on the sleeves was an additional challenge. The following order should help you:

1. Fold back facings or seam allowances on right front. (Marta's blouse has a sewn on front facing). Lap center front seamlines of blouse. Mark where rows of stitching must come together. As you can see, if they cross at center front they will not cross where blouse overlaps. To make them chevron, the angle of one front is different that the other, but a great "trompe d'oeil."

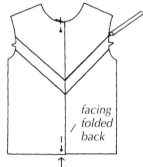

facing folded back

2. Draw a line down center of sleeve pattern. Cut along line and add seam allowances.

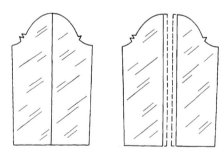

3. Next, lap **seam lines** of blouse FRONTS and sleeve FRONTS at armhole to mark where the rows of stitching must come together.

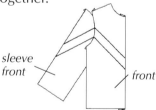

sleeve front   *front*

4. Lap sleeve fronts over sleeve backs to mark placement lines for chevron.

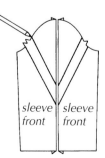

sleeve front   *sleeve front*

5. Fold and flatlock on all marked lines.

6. Join sleeve sections back together. Continue to construct blouse following pattern directions.

Marta's blouse is of handkerchief linen and she used rayon embroidery thread for the upper looper and used matching regular thread in the needle and lower looper. She shortened her stitch length to a satin stitch. Marta says the PLANNING took more time than the sewing!

Self-Fabric Piped Facing

Although Karen chose the same pattern as Lynn used for her Facile top shown on page 91, the silky polyester print and rolled edge accents give it a completely different look.

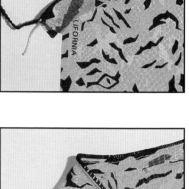

1. Serge the front panel seams with the rolled edge, wrong sides together, using a 1 mm stitch length and texturized nylon in the needle and both loopers.

2. Make serger piping (see page 58), but use bias strips of the blouse fabric instead of nylon tricot. This allows the piping to also become the facing!

3. Stitch piping to right side of neckline. Turn seam allowances to wrong side. Trim and grade if necessary. Press very lightly as texturized nylon thread can melt.

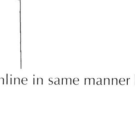

4. Topstitch just below piping through all layers to hold facing in place. There is no need to finish the facing edges as bias doesn't ravel.

5. Attach piping to lower edge of sleeve at hemline in same manner before underarm seam is sewn.

FROM DAY TO EVENING—ADD A PEPLUM!

Necessity is the mother of invention. Karen made her blouse for her Palmer/Pletsch seminars, but needed a dressier evening outfit during one of her trips. She solved the problem by making a detachable peplum from her blouse fabric. She cut the peplum from another pattern, then finished it as follows:

1. Serge-finish the top and center back edges.

2. Press under the center back seam allowances.

3. Roll edge the bottom.

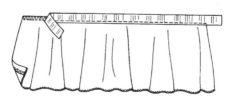

4. Cut grosgrain 2" longer than your waist measurement and topstitch to the top of peplum. Fold under ends of gros grain and sew on velcro strips to anchor them.

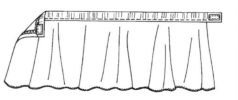

5. When wearing the peplum, the grosgrain can be covered by a belt. Karen used a dressier wide satin ribbon tied in a bow at the front.

Creative "Sweats"

T-Shirt Ribbing Tips

Since this chapter includes FOUR garments with T-shirt ribbing, it is a good time to summarize ribbing tips for you. We experimented thoroughly when we designed a sweatshirt pattern for McCall's. The following tips apply to all but sweaterknit ribbings (see page 101).

- **You can sew the ribbing in a circle** (a neater method).

  -Seam ribbing conventionally and finger-press seam open.

  -Fold in half and serge to right side of garment with ribbing on top.

SPECIAL TIPS FOR QUARTERING NECKLINE RIBBING:

-Quarter ribbing by folding in half and half again.

-Quarter neckline by matching center front and back then folding in half again

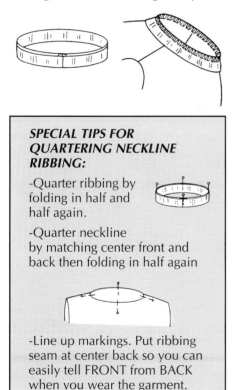

-Line up markings. Put ribbing seam at center back so you can easily tell FRONT from BACK when you wear the garment.

- **You can apply ribbing flat** (easier for children to sew):

  -Serge one shoulder seam.

  -Fold ribbing in half lengthwise wrong sides together.

  -Serge to right side of garment with ribbing on top.

  -Serge other shoulder seam through ribbing.

  -Tie a knot in tail and bury it in serger stitches with a tapestry needle.

SPECIAL TIP: To tie a knot, do it the way Pati learned in 4-H. Make a loose knot. Place a straight pin's through the center of the knot and into garment edge. Pull knot tight around pin. Voilà! The knot ends up at fabric **edge.**

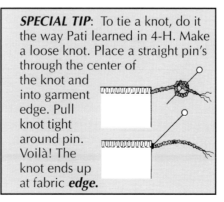

- *We prefer cotton or poly/cotton ribbing. Acrylic is too soft.*

- *Do not preshrink ribbing—it becomes too soft to handle.*

- *Ribbing should be 2-3" smaller than neckline.*

- *Cut neckline ribbing for 1 1/4" finished width as it can shrink to 1" during washings.*

- *Stretch ribbing to fit neckline and sew with ribbing on top.*

- *For even stitching, trim seam allowance to 3/8" on ribbing and garment edges.*

- *Since serged seam allowances are narrow, there is a chance of them "popping" next to the ribbing. Reinforce with a straight stitch before attaching ribbing.*

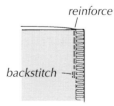

- *If unsure of fit, amount of stretch, or you are having a hard time controlling ribbing, hand or machine baste ribbing to garment first.*

- *Press ribbing as little as possible–it gets out of shape. Steaming or finger pressing is best.*

It's not made of sweatshirt fleece, but Lynn's two-piece green, white and taupe nautical stripe outfit is sure to be as comfortable as any "sweats" because it's made of 100% cotton interlock knit. It is soft, fashionable, and great when less warmth is needed. It's fast to make because nearly all the sewing was completed on the serger.

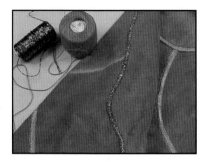

The "Ultra-Yuppie" Sweatshirt

Marta was inspired to design this patchwork sweatshirt of Ultrasuede Facile because she had some scraps she wanted to use creatively. Since the pieces are all the same color, Marta cut them without attention to nap, to yield subtle variations in shading as in real suede. She also introduced textural variety with multiple thread choices, yet all in the same "shades of rose" color family for a sophisticated tone-on-tone effect.

1. ***Draw piecing lines on the pattern tissue.*** If using scraps, plan the sizes of the pieces accordingly. Number each (in the sequence they will be sewn) and then draw a sketch to remind you how to put the "jigsaw puzzle" back together!

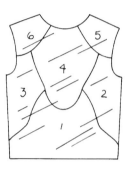

2. ***Cut the tissue into sections*** and lay the pieces on the fabric. Because sections will be joined with lapped seaming, plan where to lap pieces over or under one another. Add 1/2" seam allowances to underlap edges prior to cutting.

washable marker

3. With a 3-thread balanced stitch, ***serge the edges to be overlapped***, changing thread as often as desired for variety. (In all, Marta used seven different threads—silk buttonhole twist, Decor 6, pearl cotton #5, pearl cotton #8 together with fine metallic thread, ribbon thread, iridescent metallic ribbon thread and metallic yarn.)

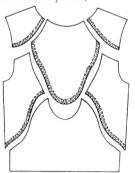

4. ***Steam-baste pieces together*** according to your sketch using narrow strips of fusible web. (See page 35.) Topstitch along edges, "burying" straight stitches in serging.

topstitch

fusible web

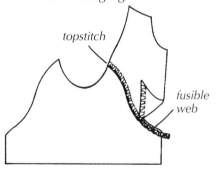

NOTE: Be sure to use press cloth when top pressing Ultrasuede Brand Fabrics.

5. Once whole garments sections are pieced, construct sweatshirt as usual.

Color-Blocked Flatlocked Sweatshirt

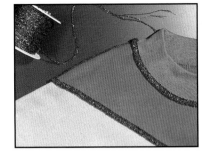

Just as scraps of Ultrasuede Facile gave Marta the idea for her patchwork sweatshirt, so too did scraps of fleece inspire her to design this color-blocked sweatshirt. She joined pieces with flatlocking, using Madeira's Lamé in the upper looper, until they "filled up" the pattern sections. From this "yardage," Marta cut out the garment. She offers these tips:

- When color blocking two colors of fabric, always serge with the same color on top. That way the same color will show through the stitching if you use a long stitch length. For example, Marta always serged with the magenta fleece on top, so that it would show through the flatlock "loops" of white thread throughout the garment.

- Trimming a little off the edge ensures the color under the stitching is even width.

- If you don't have enough ribbing for the lower edge, consider flatlock hemming it instead.

- Flatlock the ribbing to the neckline.

Lettuce-Trimmed Cocoon Cover-Up

As Palmer/Pletsch's "veteran" serger workshop instructor, Marta wanted to use the lettuce technique in a sample garment to inspire others to have fun with it. She made this cocoon jacket of a cotton T-shirt knit she had used before, so she knew how "leafy" it could be. She chose Woolly Nylon in colors to match her three colors of ribbing.

Marta successfully "lettuced" the fabric after she had finished the garment; but she admits that next time, she would lettuce before applying the ribbing. In this case, she had to start and stop as close to the ribbing seam as possible.

1. Plan placement of lettuce. (Marta's continues around from front to back.) Mark lines with vanishing marker or chalk, if desired.

2. Fold fabric on the lines, wrong sides together. Pin parallel to the fold, about an inch away.

3. With the rolled edge engaged, serge along the fold, stretching the fabric in the process.

4. Cut off tails. Dab ends of lettuce with seam sealant.

"Four-Step" Tops

The Four-Step Blouse

Marta used texturized nylon thread in both loopers for rolled edge seams to simulate piping on her silk crepe de Chine blouse. To stitch the back yoke seam, Marta placed the pieces WRONG sides together and serged with the needle in the seam line, trimming off the excess seam allowance. For the cuff, she also placed wrong sides together and serged around three edges—no grading, turning or edgestitching required. She attached cuffs to sleeves in the normal method.

The tie collar was also "rolled," but Marta feels it lost its drape as a result. The thread density of satin stitching together with the double thickness of fabric caused the edge to be heavy and coarse, rather than soft. Marta tried a longer stitch length, but found it unattractive because of the contrast between thread and fabric colors.

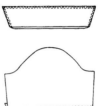

The Four-Step Camp Shirt

Handkerchief linen is perfect for a four-step blouse using a camp shirt pattern. Kathy used topstitching thread in the upper looper with her serger set for a rolled edge.

1. Roll edge the collars wrong sides together.

2. Roll edge the bottom of sleeves and top of pocket. For durability, turn up the hem and roll edge without cutting the fold. Trim excess hem allowance close to stitching.

3. Sew fronts and back to yokes.

NOTE: You can seam the back yoke with a rolled edge as long as the back isn't gathered. If there are pleats, the stitches will look different when going through the extra layers. For a 3-thread rolled edge seam to look the same on left and right fronts, you'll need to stitch both in the same direction to keep the lower looper thread on the bottom. Unfortunately, this causes rippling on the side where stitching goes against the bias.

4. Set in sleeves. Roll edge underarm seam wrong sides together. Pin front facing in place with wrong sides together. Pin collar to neckline.

5. With right side of blouse up, roll edge from lower front around neckline to lower edge of other front.

SPECIAL TIP: Machine straight stitch collar to neckline along seamline FIRST for strength. When you serge, keep roll edge stitch 1/8" away from seam line in collar area for durability.

Creative Dresses

The seams on all three dresses pictured are accented by seaming with the rolled edge or by inserting rolled edge piping. The look is the same, but the method is determined by your test sample. If a rolled edge seam doesn't look good, switch to piping...more steps, but well worth it!

Rolled Edge Accents

By choosing to accent this feminine floral print dress with rolled edging, Lynn was able to save sewing time in the process. The collar and cuffs have no enclosed seams, and the single-layer tie and hem edge of the dress were finished—all in one step—with the rolled edge to match the collar. Lynn placed rayon thread in the upper looper for its sheen, to complement the sheen of the silky polyester dress fabric.

After interfacing the collar, place the two collar sections WRONG SIDES TOGETHER. Serge around outer edges, trimming off the seam allowance at the same time. Rather than turn the corner, simply run off the edge, then start again on the next side. Secure collar points with dots of seam sealant, then cut all roll edge tails. Apply the collar to the neck edge in the usual way.

Make a thread loop to hold the tie in place under the back of the collar, just like ready-to-wear: Serge a continuous chain about 3" long, holding the thread tail lightly. With a large-eyed needle, thread both ends of the chain into the neckline seam at the center back, then knot it on the inside to secure.

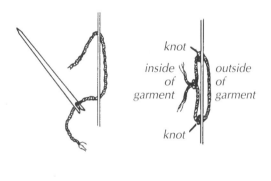

knot

inside of garment

outside of garment

knot

> NOTE: Use Woolly Nylon for a durable chain. Rayon is too fragile.

Lynn assembled and attached the cuffs following conventional methods, then stitched along the lower edges with the rolled edge engaged.

Serger Piping Outlines a Dress

Lynn's first thought for highlighting this fine yellow linen fabric was to use rolled edging with fine rayon thread as on the floral print dress, but she found the stiffness of the linen and the loose weave created too many "pokeys" which fine thread didn't cover. Texturized nylon solved that problem, but Lynn didn't care for the thread's dullness next to the matte linen. It pays to test!

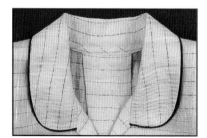

Serger piping was the answer. It enabled Lynn to use shiny, fine rayon thread in the upper looper and still achieve a solid row of satin stitching to outline the edges of the collar and pocket flaps. While you can buy pre-made black piping, the kind readily available in the stores lacks sheen and is bulky (inappropriate for this fine-weight linen).

Lynn has experimented with three methods of rolled edge piping, using 1-3 strands of filler cord like pearl cotton and strips of bias tricot like Seams Great® or Seams Saver™.

 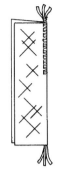 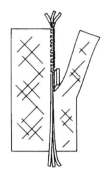

Use 5/8" tricot and serge, barely catching the edge.

Use 1 1/4" tricot folded over cording and serge through all layers.

Use 1 1/4" tricot and trim off a little. (Leave 5/8" on left side so you can easily insert piping into seam.)

Lynn prefers the fold over method. Basic serged piping steps are as follows:

1. Begin serging over filler cords for 1-2".

2. Fold tricot over cords and insert under presser foot. (Stretch tricot. Place direction that curls down toward stitch finger.)

3. Serge over tricot and filler cords. Be careful not to stitch **through** cords or you won't be able to smooth piping out.

4. Insert piping as usual using a zipper foot and stitching close to piping so tricot doesn't show. (For more serger piping tips turn to pages 23, 77 and 103. Also see our book, **Sewing With Sergers**, for additional piping instructions.)

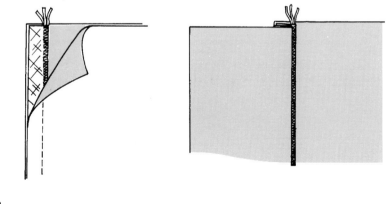

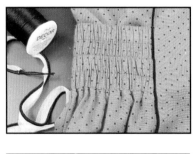

Lynn could have accented the princess lines of her blouse and the panels of her skirt by seaming with rolled edging. Why then, did she choose the multiple-step process of making and inserting piping?

Lynn says she just didn't want to take the chance that this loosely-woven polyester/rayon challis might eventually, after repeated wearing and washing, tear away from the narrow stitch. She again followed the "fold-over" method to make piping, this time using rayon Decor 6 in the upper looper.

Creative Piping Ideas

Just for fun, we have photographed some additional ideas for very creative piping you can make using the rolled edge on your serge:

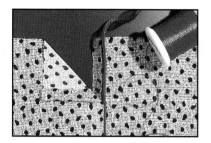

Shiny red piping used with this silky print.
Thread: Decor 6 rayon

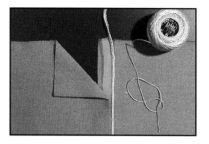

Beige wool flannel with creamy colored piping.
Thread: Pearl cotton #8

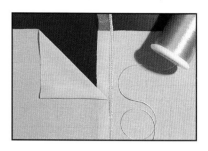

Tone-on-tone piping for a special effect.
Thread: Decor 6 rayon

Variegated piping picks up the lavender in the fabric.
Thread: Crochet thread

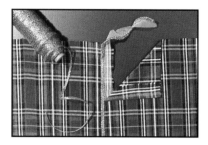

Plaid taffeta with metallic piping.
Thread: Ribbon thread

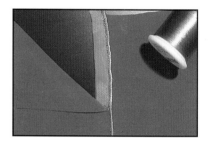

Blue silk with lighter colored shiny piping.
Thread: Decor 6 rayon

Rolled Edge "Squiggles"

"You're only limited by your imagination." It's a phrase we've often applied to creative sewing and serging, and Karen's green wool jersey dress is proof! The "squiggles" at the shoulder are not found in any book—they came out of her imagination.

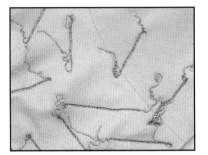

Set your serger for a rolled edge, and place Madeira's Supertwist metallic AND clear nylon in the upper looper, and clear nylon thread alone in both the needle and lower looper. Mark where you want the "squiggles," then fold the fabric wrong sides together and serge along the fold. While doing so, stretch the fabric to make it "lettuce." The combination of the metallic and the clear thread produces a wiry stitch that "squiggles up," as Karen would say. A fun touch!

NOTE: For woven fabrics, your "squiggles" will need to be on the bias for the fabric to lettuce.

Karen stabilized the shoulder seams with stay tape to prevent the wool jersey from stretching. Since she couldn't find ribbing to match the unusual color, she made self-fabric collar and cuffs. And then, as it turned out, she preferred the way the jersey created a funnel effect at the neckline.

"Outside" Facing Neckline

Serging need not contrast to be decorative! As is apparent in Lynn's two-piece maroon wool jersey dress, a matching color thread lends subtle sophistication to exposed serging. In this case, Lynn chose texturized nylon thread.

To finish the neckline:

1. Cut neckline interfacings 1/4" smaller than facing pieces on outer edges and fuse in place 1/8" from outside edge. Interfacing should not come to outer edge or it might show. Stitch shoulder seams in facings. Trim and press open.

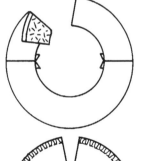

2. Using texturized nylon in the upper looper of a balanced 3-thread stitch (length 3 mm; width 5 mm), serge outside edge of facing, trimming 1/8".

3. Apply RIGHT side of facing to WRONG side of neckline. Grade, clip and turn facing to outside; press.

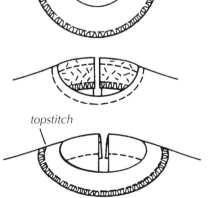

topstitch

4. Anchor outer edge of facing by topstitching on the needle line of the serger stitch.

Tone-on-Tone Flatlocked Hem

To flatlock hems so that "loops" are on the right side:

1. Fold hem allowance to the inside, press.

2. Fold in again to wrong side with raw edge firmly against second fold. From the right side, flatlock next to the fold, catching the hem allowance in the stitch at the same time. With thicker fabrics let stitches hang off the fold.

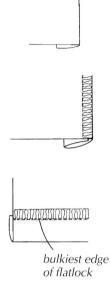

> NOTE: If you flatlock on garment side rather than having hem side on top, the bulky edge of a **3-thread** flatlock will be at the bottom.

3. Pull the hem down until stitching is flat. If you have missed a spot or two, repair by hand stitching or with dots of fusible web.

bulkiest edge of flatlock

Flatlocked Smocking

Machine smocking is easy with the serger! Elastic thread provides the stretchability that is characteristic of this decorative craft, traditionally worked by hand.

Lynn used smocking to define the waistline of this simple wool jersey top. While it may look as if the lower edge is just gathered up, there is actually a separate band for both front and back. Simply drawing up the lower edge of this top would not have given enough fullness. PLUS the fullness is much easier to control when smocking is done on a separate piece, **then** applied to garment. Each band can be stretched to arm's length to distribute the fullness evenly over the entire piece.

1. Measure waistline and cut two bands each that length. (One band will be for the front and one for the back to make double-fullness smocking.)

2. Place texturized nylon thread in the needle and loopers for strength and softness. Fold fabric right sides together and flatlock along the fold. Fold and stitch additional rows on each band, using the width of the presser foot as a spacing guide.

> NOTE: Our CREATIVE SERGING book calls for flatlocking OVER elastic cord, but Lynn found it easier to insert the cord by hand AFTER flatlocking, using a blunt pointed tapestry needle.

3. With a large tapestry needle, thread elastic through the "loops" of flatlocking on the wrong side. Allow 3" to 4" of extra elastic at each end. (See page 20 for shirring.)

4. Hold all elastic threads at BOTH ends and s-t-r-e-t-c-h to draw up fullness.

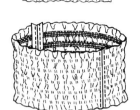

5. Join bands at side seams with a conventional straight stitch, then press seams open. To further ensure that elastic cords are held in place, topstitch close to the seam line on both sides of the seam.

Karen's yoked skirt, to wear with her wool jersey "squiggle" top, is also smocked, but her method is a bit different from Lynn's. She used two separate panels (front and back) as Lynn did, but she says it's not a true tube. Instead, Karen adjusted the fullness according to the width of her body as it increased from waist to hipline (as a yoke would be fitted).

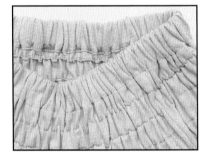

> NOTE: Karen preferred to flatlock over cord. Lynn preferred to thread cord through later.

1. Select a skirt pattern with a yoke and elastic waistline (or add a casing at the top). Add about 12" to the sides of both front and back yoke pieces.

2. Using three spools of transparent thread, flatlock (right sides together) **over** elastic cord in rows on the two yoke panels before joining them to the skirt. Leave long tails of elastic cord. (See page 23 for cording how-to's.)

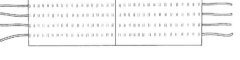

3. Seam the yokes, keeping cords free from seams. Sew side seams in skirt, then attach yoke section.

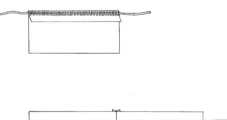

4. Knot elastic cords on one side, then pull up on opposite side to fit your body. (At the waistline they will be pulled up more than at the hipline.)

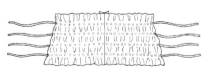

5. Sew the other side seam through elastic cords, anchoring them.

6. Make casing at waistline; insert 1" elastic and draw up to fit.

Flatlocked Items

This cool cotton knit is one of the most comfortable dresses Marta finds in her summer wardrobe. Thanks to the serger and the simple design of the two pieces, she sewed the outfit in a flash! For more interest, Marta flatlocked hems of the sleeves, pocket, and the skirt with Decor 6 rayon (loops out).

Serger Fagoting on Silk Noil

Ann has done fagoting on the conventional sewing machine, so now was motivated to create a dress with serger fagoting. She used silk noil, knowing natural fibers work well.

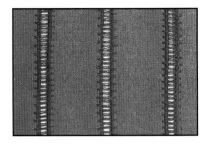

> NOTE: Serger fagoting is best on the straight of grain. Avoid it in curved areas.

Planning begins at the layout stage. For two rows of fagoting add 2 1/2" (four seam allowances) to the length of the skirt. Cut out the rest of the pieces as usual except for the bodice front.

For the bodice front, cut a full width piece of fabric the length needed for the pattern piece. Since Ann planned that a row of fagoting would go down the center, she cut the piece of fabric in half along the lengthwise grain (parallel to the selvage). Mark fabric for additional rows of fagoting, allowing for 5/8" to be turned under. Cut fabric apart.

1. Press 5/8" seam allowances to the under side.

2. Set up serger for flatlocking. Place topstitching thread in size 14/90 needle and nylon monofilament thread in both loopers. Use the widest stitch width, but test to find the stitch length you like. The longer the stitch, the more open the fagoting will be. How modest are you?!

3. Align folded edges, **right sides together**; and pin parallel to the edges, out of the way of the presser foot. Flatlock with needle barely entering the folds. (Stitches hang off the edge.)

4. Open the fabric and pull layers apart to reveal fagoting. Anchor each side with a decorative stitch (or satin stitching) on the conventional machine, pulling the fabric flat as you stitch. From under side, trim away seam allowance close to satin stitching.

5. Fold embellished piece of fabric in half, place bodice front pattern piece along fold (at center row of fagoting) and cut out.

6. Sew skirt seams. Plan placement of fagoting on skirt and cut skirt apart, parallel to the hemline. Follow steps 1-4 above for fagoting.

7. Complete dress as usual.

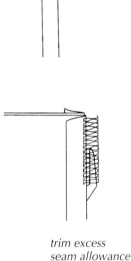

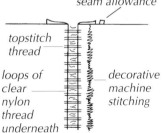

trim excess seam allowance

topstitch thread

loops of clear nylon thread underneath

decorative machine stitching

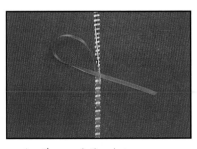

Another variation is to use a tapestry needle and thread ribbon through every other stitch, being careful not to catch the nylon loops below.

Serge Into Evening

Chanel Inspires Us Today!

The simplicity of this Chanel-inspired jacket lends itself to single-layer construction, so Lynn chose a fabric which would not need any inner construction to hold its body and shape—quilted metallic. She joined the pieces of the jacket using conventional seams, then finished the edges.

YLI's "Candlelight" gold metallic yarn is in the upper looper of the 3-thread overlock stitch, and the needle and lower looper have regular serger thread in black. As a result, the metallic serging looks "framed" on the face of the fabric, while the under side of the stitch "disappears" into the solid black back of the fabric. A smashing evening wrap that you can whip up the night before!

Evening Shell

Karen's gold metallic shell is perfect under Lynn's jacket. Karen finished the neckline and armholes with metallic yarn in the upper looper of the rolled edge stitch—no facings—so the top went together in a snap.

To prevent "pokeys" when roll hemming metallic fabrics, place a strip of sheer tricot (Seams Great, Seams Saver) ON TOP OF the fabric, then serge through all layers. Trim away excess tricot.

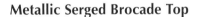

Metallic Serged Brocade Top

We've said before that the thread possibilities for the serger are virtually limitless. Even cords and yarns that don't look like machine threads may work effectively in the serger—and provide some dramatic effects! Such is the case with Madeira's #3 metallic. It comes in a package—not on a spool, cone or ball—of only 22 yards. It's labeled "metallic-effect yarn (60% metal/40% polyester) for embroidery and knitting," but there's nothing that says you can't try it in the serger! That's exactly what Marta did and you can see the result. Break the package open at the bottom and slip it on spool rod. Open the top and pull the yarn through to thread your serger.

The fabric of her evening top is a blended metallic with a woolly hand. Marta decided the edges didn't need facings, but she did stabilize the neckline with fusible knit interfacing before serging. The armhole, by contrast, is simply turned under on the seam line and then serged on the fold.

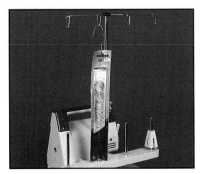

To avoid serging in circles, rearrange the sewing order:

1. First, sew the left shoulder seam, then serge the neckline, using the inside corner technique at the bottom of the "V."

Stitch until knife hits corner | *With needle in fabric, pull fabric to create straight line* | *Continue serging up other side of "V." Bottom point will be slightly rounded*

2. Next, sew the right shoulder seam, then finish the armholes.

3. Sew side seams.

4. Serge the lower edge with regular thread, then turn under and topstitch.

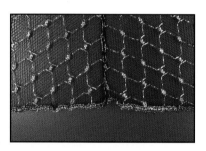

Simply Elegant Ball Gown

Pati Palmer wanted a simple but elegant dress for a formal party. She chose black velvet for this backless sheath with a flounce on the bottom. The flounce is made from taffeta and a gilded netting.

Seam the black and gold netting right sides together using a rolled edge and black thread. It is the perfect seam for such a sheer. Finish the top and bottom of the flounce with roll edging using fine gold metallic thread in the upper looper and regular black thread in the lower looper and needle.

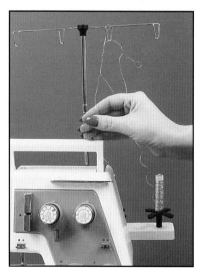

NOTE: All threads kept breaking, so Pati changed to a narrow balanced stitch which has the effect of a rolled edge. Even then, the metallic thread still kept twisting, knotting and eventually breaking as it came off the spool. To keep the thread smooth Pati let it feed through her hand just above the spool.

The top of the flounce was gathered 5/8" from the edge and topstitched onto the dress.

Pretty Rolled Edge Party Dress

The party dress Marta made for her daughter Staci was the perfect candidate for rolled edging. What other hem finish would have been as attractive— or as fast and easy—on the sheer metallic fabric of the skirt? Marta used Candlelight metallic yarn in the upper looper with the stitch length at 3 mm to accommodate the heavier thread. She also edged a strip of self-fabric in the same way, then gathered it up to create the rosette accessory (see page 71 for instructions).

roll hem on flower and sleeve

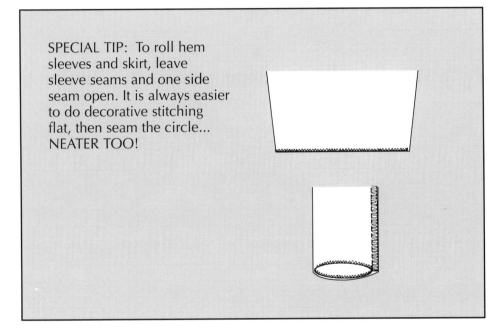

SPECIAL TIP: To roll hem sleeves and skirt, leave sleeve seams and one side seam open. It is always easier to do decorative stitching flat, then seam the circle... NEATER TOO!

Romancing Velvet and Chiffon

Velvet and chiffon are synonymous with special occasions, but would either of them bring "serging" to your mind? As Marta's handkerchief-point dress exemplifies, both fabrics, though very different from each other, can be decoratively serged for gorgeous results. You just have to TEST for the right thread!

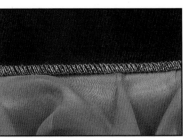

floppy rosette

The chiffon skirt is attached at the hipline to a full length satin slip. Marta had intended to use gold metallic thread to roll hem the chiffon, but absolutely couldn't make it work. It was too stiff. She finally settled on 40 wt. silk thread that matched the chiffon and used a 4 mm stitch length and was very pleased with the look. 40wt rayon would also work. To turn the corners, Marta raised the presser foot, slipped the stitches off the stitch finger, turned the corner, and began stitching at the top edge.

In a needlepoint store, Marta found a special thread to use on the rayon/silk velvet. Distributed by Balger, the thread is 67% rayon and 33% polyester and has an iridescent quality. Marta used it in the upper looper of a wide 3-thread balanced stitch, to serge on the SINGLE layer at the neck, sleeve and lower edges.

metallic thread on velvet

To make the huge, floppy rosette:

1. Cut a strip of chiffon (8" X 36"). Roll hem the edges with the stitch length set at 4 mm. (The longer stitch is more desirable on chiffon. With a short stitch the hem will pull away from the chiffon.)

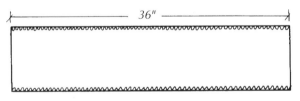

roll edged chiffon

2. Fold it nearly in half lengthwise.

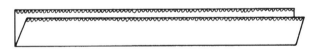

3. Gather the strip along folded edge.

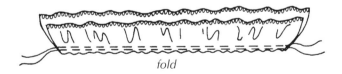

fold

4. Gather into the shape of a flower.

5. Sew a velvet-covered button in the center.

Flatlocking Silkies

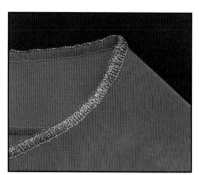

Lynn and Marta each made an evening top combining various colors of silky polyester fabrics, which they pieced together by flatlocking with metallic yarn in the upper looper. They each used a sweatshirt pattern with a raglan sleeve to camouflage the sleeve seam.

1. Start with four different half-yard lengths of fabric. Sketch how you want to piece them for an interesting design, then plan the sewing order to avoid getting "stuck" in a corner.

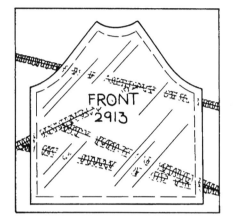

2. Create pieced "yardage" by joining the pieces with flatlocking, then cut out your garment.

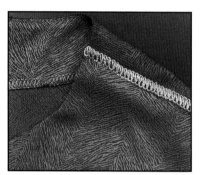

3. Sew shoulder seams. Face the neckline conventionally, as Lynn did. Or, as on Marta's, decoratively serge facing to garment wrong sides together, trimming off seam allowance as you serge.

4. Attach the sleeves with flatlocking to match the piecing. Serge along the single layer to finish the sleeve and hem edges.

NOTE: We don't usually recommend flatlocking on woven fabrics without additional stabilization, but the loose fit of this garment and the limited wear it will endure lessen the need for durability. Use the widest stitch to catch as much fabric as possible in the flatlock seam. Do a test first, as Marta and Lynn did. Pull on the seams to check stability.

The Ultimate Evening Suit with Custom Passementerie Trim

Passementerie, defined as trims on garments, is all the rage in fashion now, and the serger provides the means to fashion your own custom trims—no more endless shopping trips looking for just the right color and style. Marta trimmed her evening suit with custom braid she created from Decor 6 rayon thread and Candlelight metallic yarn on a base of Seams Great.

1. Serge along one edge of 5/8" or 1 1/4" Seams Great or Seams Saver using a rolled edge with a medium stitch length and Decor 6 in the upper looper. Place edge that curls down against presser foot.

2. Convert your machine to a 3-thread balanced stitch at the widest stitch width. With metallic yarn in the upper looper and a satin stitch length, serge other side of Seams Great, butting stitch against the rolled edge. Trim Seams Great only if necessary.

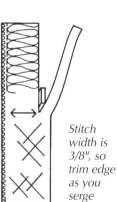

Stitch width is 3/8", so trim edge as you serge

3. Position trim on garment and hand stitch in place.

For her hook loops on front opening Marta created matching narrow braid by serging a rolled edge chain of the same thread.

Formal Fantasy with Rolled Edge Metallic Piping

Pati is ready for the ballroom in this elegant dress of polyester faille, a look she copied from a designer gown she had seen in "W" magazine. The rolled edge piping (metallic yarn in the upper looper) provides all the embellishment.

Outline the neckline and waistline with serger piping, and hem the skirt in one step by simply roll hemming.

To make metallic piping, use 3 strands of pearl cotton #8 (the finer one).

1. Serge a rolled edge over the cording alone for 1-2" with Candlelight metallic yarn from YLI in the upper looper and regular thread in the lower looper and needle.

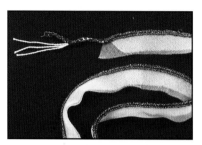

2. Fold 1 1/4" Seams Great or Seams Saver (see page 58) over cording.

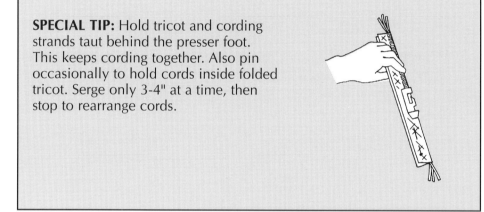

SPECIAL TIP: Hold tricot and cording strands taut behind the presser foot. This keeps cording together. Also pin occasionally to hold cords inside folded tricot. Serge only 3-4" at a time, then stop to rearrange cords.

ANOTHER SPECIAL TIP: If piping stretches, try differential feed set at 2 to prevent curling. If you don't have differential feed, simply press finished piping to make it lie flat.

3. Note that piping has a right and wrong side. Insert piping into seam using zipper foot on conventional machine so you can stitch close to piping. You need to catch the edge of the metallic threads so the tricot doesn't show. Also note that the piping has a right and wrong side. Check before inserting into seams.

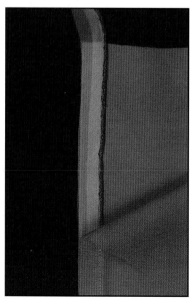

Metallic piping takes patience and practice, but next time your machine is set at a rolled edge, get out your Seams Great or Seams Saver and try it! The finished look is unusually beautiful and not found ready-made.

See pages 23, 58, 59 and 103 for more piping ideas and tips.

Serging for Swim and Aerobics

The Fabrics, Elastics and Linings

We have noticed more and more fashion-sewers are making their own leotards, tights and swimsuits since the advent of serging. If you've never made them yourself, give them a try! You'll be pleasantly surprised to discover how easy, fast and fun they are to sew. With a little practice, you can whip one up in less than two hours.

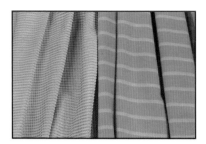

Fabrics: When patterns specify "for two-way stretch swimwear knits only," look for fabrics with spandex such as Lycra®. To test the stretch of your fabric, fold over several inches of fabric along one edge. Stretch the fabric and measure, using the knit gauge on the pattern envelope. Repeat for opposite edge of fabric.

Lycra spandex may be blended with nylon or cotton or with both cotton and polyester. The blends have excellent stretchability and shape retention (wet or dry), which make them excellent choices for swimwear. Nylon/Lycra is shiny and is available in a wide range of vibrant colors. It dries very quickly, a swimwear plus.

Lycra blended with cotton is relatively new on the home-sewing market. It has a matte finish and is easier to sew than the more slippery nylon/Lycra. In addition, the cotton content absorbs moisture from the body to keep you cool, making it an excellent choice for sunbathing or aerobics. Once wet, however, cotton/Lycra does not dry as quickly as nylon/Lycra.

Lining: Choose a two-way stretch swim lining. It is available from Sew Easy Lingerie (wholesale only) or Jantzen Fabric Outlet in Portland, Oregon (by mail order). Again, check the stretch in both directions using the knit gauge on the pattern envelope. We prefer beige as it is closer to skin tones. If you're unable to find two-way stretch swim lining in your fabric store, self-fabric can be used with good results. If self-fabric shows through to the right side, pick a solid nylon/Lycra or cotton/Lycra to use as a lining. Avoid one-way stretch knits for swimsuit lining. They will alter the fit of the suit.

Elastic: Choose elastic that is specifically recommended for swimwear. We use and recommend **cotton braid swimwear elastic** for its durability. It retains its stretchability when stitched through and its shape when wet. It comes in a variety of widths and is usually sold by the yard off large spools.

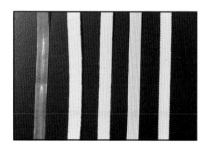

From left to right: clear elastic, cotton braid, polyester braid, nylon braid and polyester knit elastic.

A new clear elastic has recently become available and is working well for us.

Other elastics suitable for swimwear are polyester braid, nylon braid and polyester knit elastic. **We recommend them in the order listed.** Avoid acetate elastic for swimwear. It loses its shape when wet—you may lose your suit!

Be sure to use the correct width elastic as called for in the pattern instructions. Each width has a different amount of stretch and is not interchangeable without altering the fit. Generally, 3/8" elastic is used.

Let's look at some actual garments and see what a difference your serger can make in this activewear grouping:

The Creative Maillot With Lettuce Edge

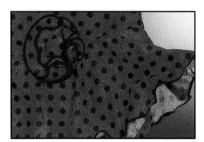

Had Lynn made this swim suit exactly as the pattern envelope showed, it would have been cute. But doesn't her added lettuce edge and "rosette" to match add that much more to its appeal? Use your serger creatively!

Lynn used texturized nylon for all three threads to provide strength in the stretchy seams and softness next to the skin. The regular 3-thread overlock (2.5 mm stitch length) joins the seams, while the rolled edge is engaged for the lettuce.

Because of their stretch capacity, nylon/spandex fabrics are ideal for the lettuce edge. The shorter the stitch length, the more ruffling you'll get. Increasing the presser foot pressure also helps, but most of all you just need to S-T-R-E-T-C-H the fabric as much as possible while the MACHINE FEEDS it through. (Caution: Don't pull the fabric through the machine or you may bend or break the needle or loopers.)

Lynn used the new clear elastic of 100% polyurethane because it is less bulky and because it is not weakened if you happen to cut into it with the serger knives. Apply elastic for a ready-to-wear look, as follows:

1. Cut elastic to the length suggested by the pattern or fit it to your body area by "trying on" the elastic. Standard ratios for length of elastic to fabric are 1:1 at neckline and armholes, 1:1 at the front leg and 3:4 at the back leg (or about 2" less elastic than fabric). This allows the elastic to "cup" the fabric under the fanny.

2. Set the stitch length at 4 mm as stitches will be closer when the elastic contracts. Serge elastic to wrong side of fabric. Take a couple stitches into elastic before you begin to stretch it to fit the fabric. Hold (DON'T PULL) all layers behind the foot with your left hand as you serge. Use your right hand to stretch the elastic to fit the opening. Work just an inch or two at a time to distribute the stretch evenly.

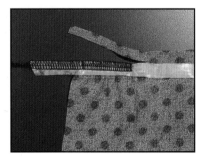

NOTE: Guide elastic 1/8" in from edge of fabric and trim off fabric extension as you stitch. If you try to guide the elastic at the fabric edge, it is too easy for the fabric to shift as you serge without your knowing it, resulting in a few spots where the fabric doesn't get caught in the stitching.

4. Turn the serged edge to the inside, enclosing the elastic. With your conventional machine set on a long stitch (8 to 10 stitches to the inch), topstitch 1/4" to 3/8" from the edge through all layers, stretching as you sew.

NOTE: For a ready-to-wear look and a topstitch that stretches, use a twin needle (size 2.0/80). Because the two needle threads share one bobbin, the under side resembles a zigzag stitch.

The Blouson Swim Suits Any Figure

Marta's swimsuit is also of nylon/spandex fabric, which she seamed with texturized nylon thread. Marta prefers regular swimsuit elastic to the clear elastic that Lynn used, but she applied it using the same method. She finished the neckline and armhole edges differently, however, by binding them with strips of self fabric as the pattern had instructed.

NOTE: Palmer & Pletsch swimsuit patterns offer you special help to make your sewing easier. (A new design each year—collect them all as they are classics.) They include elastic guides so you **CAN** serge your elastic on and avoid a "homemade" casing look. PLUS! They include fitting information. Look for Personalized Instruction patterns by Palmer & Pletsch in the McCall's catalog.

Kids' Aerobics

Karen and Lynn say sewing with a friend can be fun and educational. Together they made identical kids' aerobic sets with contrast serging on the outside. They used texturized nylon for all three threads, shortening the stitch length to 1 mm for better coverage—a more solid-color look.

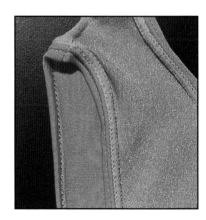

One is shown right side out, the other is worn inside out—and looks just as good!

Follow the same method for attaching elastic as described for Lynn's swimsuit, EXCEPT, serge the elastic to the *right side* of the knit. To finish, turn the edge to the OUTSIDE and topstitch with a double needle over the exposed contrast serging. Decoratively serge neckline and armhole edges, without elastic, then turn them to the outside and topstitch.

Neckline and armhole edges, without elastic, were simply decoratively serged, then turned to the outside and topstitched.

Fabulous Flatlocked Furs

The Penguin Jacket

The penguin-print "fur" itself was enough to inspire Marta to create this unusual jacket. She chose to hand knit the sleeves, to avoid an overly bulky look that would have resulted from using all fur. Alternatively, you could machine knit the sleeves, or simply buy knit or woven yardage to coordinate.

Fur is too bulky to be sewn with a regular serged seam; so use the flatlock stitch to simulate the furrier's technique of butting the edges and stitching from side to side:

1. Trim away the seam allowances. Brush fur away from the edges toward the garment, and place pieces right sides together. Flatlock, with stitches hanging off edge slightly.

2. Pull the two pieces to open flat. On the right side, carefully pull out any fur caught in the seam. A blunt pointed tapestry needle is ideal.

tapestry needle

Attach the collar and sleeves to the jacket with a regular serged seam. Sew in the sleeve lining by hand.

To finish the front edge, set stitch width to a narrow 1.5 mm and set tension dials so upper looper thread (topstitching thread) "wraps" the edge. The "fluff" of the fur camouflages the stitch.

The unfinished lower edge doesn't show because the nap, running down, covers it. Marta chose to leave it raw because there's no risk of raveling and any kind of edge finish would have disturbed the nap.

Lingerie and Sleepwear

The "Lanz Look" Mother/Daughter Nightgown

Pearl cotton's soft, fuzzy quality makes it the ideal accent for mother/daughter flannel nightgowns. Lynn was the designer who modified the pattern's instructions to eliminate facings in favor of decoratively serged edges.

1. Cut two of each yoke piece, serge fronts to backs at shoulder seams to create two yokes. Place them **wrong sides together**, then treat them as one.

2. Align bound edge of pre-gathered eyelet trim along seam line of neck opening. Machine baste.

3. With pearl cotton (Lynn used #5) in the upper looper, serge with a balanced stitch, trimming off **entire** seam allowance in the process. Use a short stitch length and the widest width possible to completely cover trim's binding.

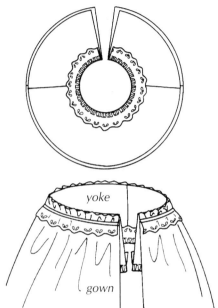

4. After joining sleeves to body of gown, run two lines of machine basting along top edge. Pin yoke to body, wrong sides together, gathering body to fit. Glue stick or machine baste wrong side of eyelet trim to right side of **gown**.

5. Decoratively serge yoke to gown, from gown side, over edge of eyelet trim.

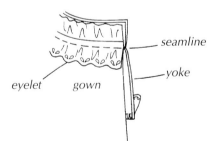

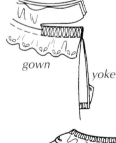

6. Press seam toward yoke. Topstitch seam allowance flat through decorative serging, "burying" straight stitches in outer edge of serging. It's now neat, tidy, soft and durable on the inside.

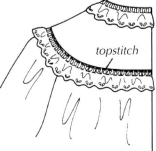

"Scalloped and Shelled" Nightgown

Marta seamed her nightgown with the ***rolled edge stitch*** set at a 3 mm length for softness on the inside. She finished the upper back bodice and hem edges with a shell edge, as follows:

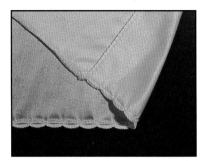

1. Serge hems with a rolled edge set at a medium stitch length (3 mm—a shorter length adds more thread at the edge, creating a coarser, heavier edge.) Tricot won't ravel, so will look neat.

2. Stitch serged hem with a "shell" stitch on the conventional machine (use the blind hem stitch or, if your machine has a blanket stitch, try that for a prettier look).

blind hem stitch: _ _ /\ _ _ /\ _ _ /\ _ _ /\ _ _   *blanket stitch:* _ _ || _ _ || _ _ || _ _ || _ _

SPECIAL TIP: Guide the rolled edge under the presser foot so the "swing" stitch just barely goes over the edge, pulling it in to create a scallop look.

Serged Lace in Charmeuse

When you can't find lace trim wide enough to suit your needs, create your own from narrower trims, as Lynn did for her camisole of bias cut polyester charmeuse. The flatlock stitch butts the edges perfectly to make it all look like one piece of wide lace trim. And when flatlocking is done with right sides together (ladders out), the stitches are unnoticeable within the lace design. Lynn used flatlocking on the matching half slip as well.

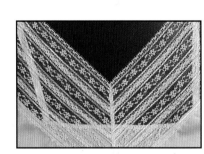

1. Sew the elastic to the right side of the fabric at waistline using a slightly longer stitch length and stretching elastic to fit fabric (stitch length appears shorter when elastic contracts).

right side knit

NOTE: For wovens, fold the seam allowance to the wrong side for added strength and flatlock elastic to fabric without cutting the fold.

right side woven

---

2. Pull to flatten seam. VOILÀ! No bulky seam allowance at waistline.

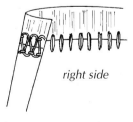

right side

At the lower edge of both slip and camisole, Lynn serged to prevent raveling, then straight stitched a narrow hem. Finally, she flatlocked lace trim to the hems, again placing right sides together for ladders out.

Woman's Lace Trimmed Peignoir

Polyester charmeuse is ideal for an elegant, but washable, gown and robe. And flatlocking is perfect for lingerie because it produces flat, non bulky seams.

Marta used 3-thread flatlocking to attach lace to all areas of the gown and robe, with Ribbon Thread in the upper looper and regular thread in the needle and lower looper.

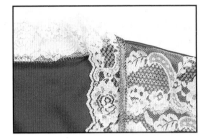

To attach lace to top of **gown** front:

1. Pin wrong side of lace to right side of gown. Fold gown wrong sides together along edge of lace. Flatlock, not cutting the fold.

2. Pull flat. Turn under 1/4" at top edge of charmeuse twice and topstitch edge of lace to fabric.

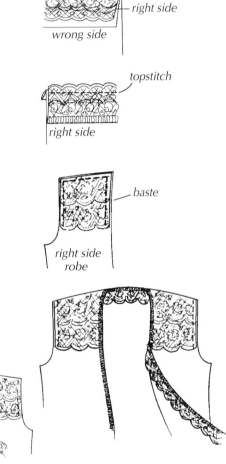

On robe attach lace yoke and lace edging to charmeuse at same time:

1. Baste two rows of wide scalloped lace to right sides of fronts, forming a "yoke."

2. Sew fronts to back at shoulder seams.

3. Place wrong side of narrow lace to wrong side of charmeuse along neck and front opening. Flatlock.

4. Pull fabric and lace front.

Man's Classic Piped Plaid Robe

Decorative serging looks equally appropriate on this elegant man's robe as on any woman's garment. Marta combined brushed cotton blend plaid with the same polyester charmeuse as on the woman's peignoir set, then highlighted the details with serged piping of Decor 6 rayon thread.

Yards and yards of piping were needed to accent front, sleeve and pocket edges of the robe. Marta used yarn as a filler cord to make thicker piping to correspond with the fabric's heavier look, and used Decor 6 in the upper looper and textured nylon in the lower looper. She decided on a medium stitch length to prevent the thread from stacking.

The monogram on the breast pocket was made from a "rolled edge chain" of Decor 6 thread over yarn. (See Tips for Handling Cording, page 23.) Simply "chain off" without fabric and hand-tack the chain of thread on the pocket in the shape of the letter desired.

Ultimate Ultrasuede®

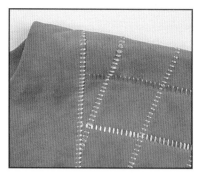

Flatlocked Ladder Interest

We've fallen in love with Ultrasuede® Facile® and have used this luscious fabric several places throughout the book. Lynn decided to try criss-cross flatlocking with the ladders out like she did on her silky blouse (page 47). She used Decor 6 thread in the needle and chose the subtle sophistication of a tone-on-tone color story.

Lynn's top has a center panel. The side panel and sleeves are cut all-in-one. You could add this same seam to any simple top with a cut-on sleeve if you wanted to copy Lynn's idea.

1. Cut out the blouse. Mark flatlocking lines on **wrong** side of fabric, since you want the "ladder" on the right side.

washable marker

2. Fold right sides together on vertical lines first and flatlock on the fold from the wrong side using a 4 mm stitch length and letting stitches hang slightly over the edge.

3. To serge horizontal lines, begin at cut edge. Since you will be ending in the middle of the fabric, release the chain from the stitch finger and chain off as on page 153.

4. Flatlock the front and side panels together from wrong side so ladder will show on right side.

NOTE: If you flatlock the seam with the needle in the seam line, then pull the seam flat, the garment width will be increased by approximately 1/4" per seam. If exact fit is **crucial** take a wider flatlock seam, increasing it by half the stitch width or about 1/8".

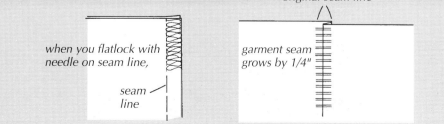

when you flatlock with needle on seam line,

seam line

original seam line

garment seam grows by 1/4"

Serging Sweaterknits

Sweaterknits are increasing in popularity because the serger makes them easy to sew. Your first project might be to recycle a sweater currently in your wardrobe, as Karen Dillon did for the child's cardigan. You can also create your own sweater yardage by hand or machine knitting, then cut and serge into a garment. Another option is to buy a sweater body kit. These are made by machine complete with ribbing at the lower edges. They come in sets for front, back and sleeve, and usually have a strip of matching ribbing to sew onto the neckline. Sweater yardage can also be purchased. We have included examples of each in the sweater section.

Recycling a Sweater

Imagine a sweater with a moth hole or permanent stain on the front. What to do? Take a suggestion from Karen who copied a look from Esprit, one of the hottest ready-to-wear names going, to create this sweater remodel. With coordinating plaid fabric, she was able to transform the flawed sweater into an adorable vest look for a child. Before sewing see page 101 for more sweaterknit sewing tips.

1. Select a child's cardigan pattern.

2. Cut sleeves and neck ribbing off old sweater. Cut front and back apart. Cut back of child's cardigan out of back of sweater. Cut back neck ribbing for child's cardigan from sweater back neck ribbing. (This eliminates the need for a back neck facing.)

3. Cut ribbing for the lower front of cardigan from FRONT sweater ribbing to match front waist measurement on pattern.

4. Cut child's sleeves from sweater.

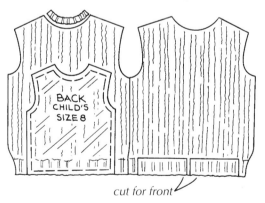

cut for front

5. Divide ribbing and back neckline into quarters. Pin rib to neckline, distributing neckline fullness evenly.

6. Before stitching stretch ribbing to fit neckline. Then release. The ribbing will return to its original size, "grabbing" the neckline along with it, easing it to fit. Machine baste WITHOUT stretching ribbing.

7. Serge over basting, trimming garment edge slightly. Do not trim ribbing edge.

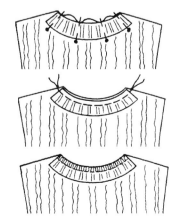

8. Cut cardigan front from plaid fabric.

9. Sew ribbing (in same manner as neckline ribbing) to lower edge of fronts, making sure length of side fronts equals side backs. Remember—DON'T stretch the ribbing while sewing!

10. Cut front facing pieces to extend below bottom edge of ribbing; interface. Sew facings to fronts, turning up lower edge.

11. Trim, turn and edgestitch.

12. Serge shoulder seams.

turn up lower edge

13. Set in sleeves. Serge underarm and sleeve seams in one step.

14. Sew buttonholes and add buttons.

Sweaterknit Yardage

Freeform" is the word we use to describe the sweater-knit appliqué on Marta's dark blue chambray top. She **hand knit** (but could have machine knit) the 30" by 12" piece, laid it diagonally across the front bodice, then cut the chambray to "frame" the knit. Here are the steps Marta followed to appliqué:

1. Mark on fabric where inset will be. Cut on those lines.

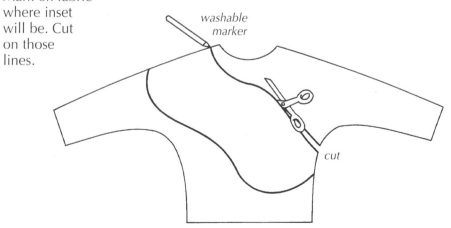
washable marker

cut

94

2. Interface edges of chambray that
    will be stitched to sweater knit
    using 1" strips of fusible knit
    interfacing.

3. Serge the chambray with #8
    pearl cotton in the upper
    looper using a 3-thread
    balanced stitch.

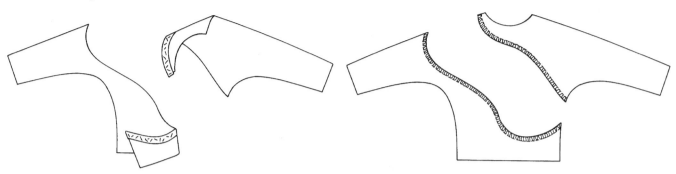

4. Lay the serged chambray edges
    onto the knit and topstitch along
    the INSIDE edge of the serging,
    "burying" the straight stitches.

5. From the underside, serge
    away excess knit with a
    regular 3-thread stitch.

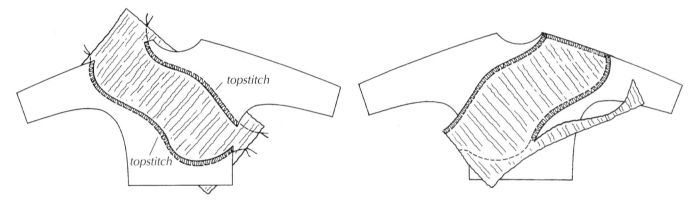

topstitch

topstitch

6. To make edge of chambray
    lie flat, topstitch again
    along the OUTSIDE edge of
    the serging, catching edge
    of loops.

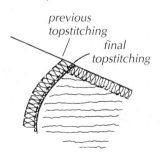

*previous
topstitching*

*final
topstitching*

Machine Knitting

Knitting machines are becoming more and more popular as an addition to the sewing room. The ability to design and create your own original yardage is exciting and with virtually unlimited possibilities. Even the most simple inexpensive machine can produce fast, stunning results in yardage to cut and serge.

Knitting machines range in yarn capabilities from the bulky hand knit look to the standard gauge, which uses fine baby weight fingering and sport weight yarn.

Single bed machines produce single knit fabric with many texture and design variations, such as tuck, fairisle (2-color knitting), and lace. The addition of a ribber or the purchase of a double bed machine increases the stitch capabilities to include ribbings as well as beautiful double knit fabrics, such as fisherman ribs and jacquards.

With the speed of knitting machines and sergers and the combination of knits and wovens you can certainly enhance your wardrobe with that original designer touch.

Sweater Panels Made on a Knitting Machine

Our resident knitting machine expert and author of **Timely Treasures**, Terri Burns (inset photo), uses her knitting machine to make wonderful creations for her twin boys (Chris in green, Philip in red). Here they model this year's Christmas outfits—sweats embellished with machine knit Santa designs.

After knitting the panels, Terri flatlocks them to ready-made sweats using knitting machine yarn in the upper looper on her serger.

1. Flatlock panels on the fold to sweatshirt front only.

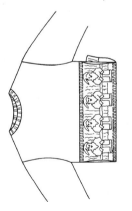

2. Turn corners (see page 119) and flatlock ends, OR open sweatshirt side seams, slip panel into seam, and re-stitch on serger.

Terri Burns, wearing her machine knit double bed four-color jacquard. Neckline edge is serged with dress yarn over clear elastic.

3. To attach panels to sweatpants, flatlock long edges as above. Turn under upper and lower edges and topstitch conventionally.

Sweater Yardage—by the Bolt

Pati was lucky enough to find this striking wool fabric and coordinating sweater knit yardage, providing interplay among plaids, stripes, geometrics and floral designs. Together, she and Kathy designed the pant and sweater jacket duo. Kathy suggested the exaggerated length for the jacket both for a fashion-forward look and to take advantage of the large design of the sweater knit.

Kathy used a basic jacket pattern with a cut-on sleeve which created a "chevron" effect where the stripes came together at the wrist. She then made bands of self-fabric—the solution when you cannot find ribbing to match your sweater knit. (In this case, Pati and Kathy could have used black ribbing, but liked the effect of the self-fabric because of the striped design.)

Stretch the straight band a little when shaping it around the curved neckline, but not when going down the front or distortion will occur. The bands should also be stretched when applied to the sleeves and at the hemline to make those sections of the garment hug the body.

Kathy and Pati recommend basting the entire jacket together before serging, both to check the fit and overall appearance (with shoulder pads in place) and to be sure the ribbings are applied evenly. Basting is much easier to rip out and re-stitch than serging! Once you are satisfied with the total look, then go to your machine and serge away!

With such a bulky knit, use the widest possible stitch to catch more knit in the seam. If you have differential feed, set it on 2 or "ease plus" to prevent stretching of seams while you sew (see page 12).

Sweater Bodies

The new White serger model 216 inspired Marta to try quilting with the decorative chain stitch. To date, it is the only chain stitch model that can accommodate heavier specialty thread in the chain looper AND also allow chain stitching far away from the edge, into the center of the fabric.

Marta chose to apply the technique to a jacket with a lower body and sleeves made from a sweater body and a quilted yoke of Ultrasuede® Facile. Marta's jacket pattern didn't have a yoke, so she cut the pattern where she wanted to make the seam then added seam allowances.

To quilt the Facile, purchase the lightest-weight quilt batting by the yard. Plan the quilting lines, being sure they will come together at the center front, and mark them with chalk. Using lots of pins to hold the Facile and batting in place, chain stitch through both with topstitching thread in the chain looper. (If your serger cannot do this, simply topstitch conventionally.) Since the chain forms on the under side, place Facile down, against the throat plate.

Marta lined the jacket with polyester lining fabric and bound the front and neckline with crosswise strips of Facile. Finally, she cuffed the sleeves with Facile, making the cuffs large enough to slip over the hand, but with elastic inside so they'll hug the wrist.

A Unique Way to Use a Sweater Body

No one said a sweater body is limited to life as a sweater, as Lynn's "ski togs" for a child illustrate. There was just enough length of patterned knit for a baby-sized body, sleeves and pant legs. Lynn joined all seams with texturized nylon for strength and softness and used the 4-thread overlock (mock safety) stitch because of its wider width to secure the bulky acrylic knit.

Lynn used the separate ribbing provided with the sweater body to make the single-layer ribbing at the neckline. It was finished on one edge and heavy enough without being doubled. To form the elastic casing at the waistline, she followed the mock band technique.

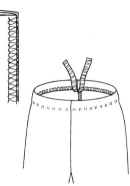

1. Adjust serger for flatlocking (5 mm width; 4 mm length). Fold casing allowance to the inside, then fold both layers to the outside as for sewing a blind hem. Serge along the fold, leaving an opening. Pull flat.

2. Insert elastic, then serge opening closed.

SPECIAL TIPS FOR SWEATER BODIES

We found there was GREAT interest in sweater bodies when we made them available during our serger workshops. The renewed interest is because of sergers. Here are a few tips and some information about sweater bodies:

- They usually come in kits with large panels with ribbing already knitted to the bottom of each. They also include a strip of matching ribbing for the neckline which is usually finished on one side so it can be used single layer or folded in half and used double if more body is desired.

- For all sweaterknits, it is recommended that you preshrink in the manner you plan to launder. 100% acrylic sweater bodies are most common, easy to handle, and inexpensive. 100% cotton sweater bodies are fairly expensive, but comfortable to wear. Cotton sweaterknits tend to grow during wear, but usually tighten back up after machine washing and drying.

- Do not preshrink neckline ribbing.

- To cut, stretch rib at lower edge to the same width as the sweaterknit and pin into your cutting board. Cut pattern pieces from underarm straight down following a rib in the sweaterknit.

- With patterned knits, match pattern at underarm seams, laying out bodies first, then sleeves.

- Sew neckline ribbing with ribbing on top. Do not stretch ribbing during sewing, as it will not recover well. Stretch **before** sewing, then release. Ribbing will ease neckline to fit for you. Now baste in place, then serge, trimming a little of neckline, but nothing from ribbing.

General tips for sewing sweaterknits:

- Preshrink washables, steam dry cleanables. Do not pretreat ribbings, it makes them too soft to handle.

- Do not touch iron to sweaterknits. They get a flat overpressed look. Steam only, holding iron above fabric and finger press seams flat if necessary. **Never** steam ribbings.

- It may be easier to cut sweaterknits using a full front and back pattern piece. Place your pattern on a folded piece of paper lining up center front and backs along fold. Cut. VOILÀ! Full front and back pattern pieces.

paper

FRONT 1612

BACK 1612

- Do not allow excess fabric to hang over cutting table—it will stretch and cause you MAJOR problems.

- Pattern weights work better than pins—they don't get lost in the bulk of the fabric!

- For more control and neater serged seams, cut 1" seam allowances on side, sleeve, and shoulder seams so you can trim as you serge. The wider seam allowances give you more control.

- Cut 3/8" seam allowances wherever you will be attaching ribbing. It's easier to control and to get ribbed bands an even width.

- Serge sweaterknits with a wide (6 mm) stitch and a 3-4 mm stitch length.

- Sew with a stable seam to prevent rippling. Terri Burns, our knitting machine expert, often uses the 4/2-thread stitch as the chain stabilizes the seam. She now has a serger with differential feed and she finds she can use nearly any stitch type for a ripple-free seam.

- To prevent stretch, use differential feed set at 2 (see page 12) or "ease plussing".

- Stabilize sweaterknit shoulder seams and any other seams that will have stress by serging over twill tape, StaTape, Seams Great or, our preference, clear elastic. Use your pattern to cut the correct length.

- If unsure of fit, stretchiness of ribbing, or evenness of finished width, hand or machine baste ribbing on first. Check the look and fit before serging.

- To attach ribbing, mark quarters (or eighths) on ribbing and neckline (see Special Tip, page 51). Pin, easing garment to fit rib. Serge, trimming garment seam allowance, but NOT rib edge. DO NOT stretch rib! Use a longer stitch length (3-4 mm) since short stitch lengths have more thread, and the more thread, the more the seam will stretch out and **remain** stretched out.

NOTE: Ribbing is generally cut 2-3" smaller than a round neckline. However, there are FEW rules to cutting the right size of sweaterknit ribbing for a neckline because the degree of stretch varies greatly. Hand basting it to neckline allows you to check size and fit. Does the ribbing look too large or too small? If so, adjust, then serge.

- If ribbing is unavailable, use self fabric as ribbing or face the neckline, or serge the raw edge, stabilizing it with strips of fusible knit applied to the wrong side, or by serging over cording (see pg.23). REMEMBER, cording doesn't stretch, so make sure the neckline will fit over your head.

- See pages 51 and 100 for more ribbing and sweaterknit tips.

Jackets WITH OUTSIDE DECORATIVE SERGING

Piping

Piping is a decorative detail all by itself, but it can serve the additional purpose of highlighting interesting seaming. The princess seaming in both front and back of Pati's linen suit might have gone unnoticed were it not for the contrast piping.

Pati chose to make her own piping using Decor 6 rayon thread in the upper looper. This gave her a fine shiny black piping not easily found. Since piping tends to "curl" up during stitching, you'll need to run your hand along entire strip to smooth it out. Now comes the confession—PATI PALMER stitched **through** her cording in one spot, so couldn't smooth it out! Ooops! She put it where she could cover it with a flower. (And during photography our model put the flower on the other side!) That's okay, Pati—nice to know you're not perfect. Pati says, "We don't sew through our cording any more though, because we've discovered better ways of doing it—see page 23." Also see pages 58, 59 and 77 for more piping instructions.

Decorative Ladders and Flatlock Tucks

Marta's pink silk suit is accented with two variations of flatlocking with "ladders out." Along the front of the jacket, the fabric lies flat, while the sleeve features tiny tucks. She used silk buttonhole twist in the needle and a 1 mm stitch length for a nearly solid row of stitching. See page 18 for more on flatlocking.

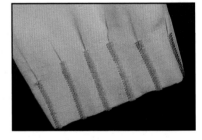

1. Before applying facings, fold fabric right sides together along front and collar. Flatlock with loops hanging over the edge, so fabric has room to flatten completely.

2. For sleeves, however, serge exactly along fold (don't cut the edge!) to create the tucks.

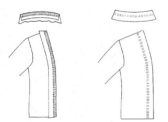

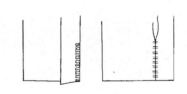

Blanket Stitch Edging

The serger blanket stitch proved to be an ideal alternative to fold over braid for edging Marta's short jacket. Pokeys are not a concern on ravel-resistant wool coating, and the contrasting decorative stitch harmonizes with the ensemble's European character.

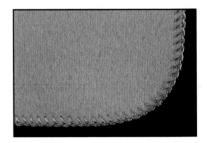

Set your serger for the 3-thread stitch with the widest width and longest length (4-5 mm). Tighten both looper tensions and loosen the needle tension until the looper threads run in a straight line along the edge of the fabric and the needle thread shows on right and wrong side.

Marta found she had to take her needle thread (Decor 6) completely out of the tension disk to loosen it enough. To tighten her lower looper tension enough, she switched to texturized nylon thread. She held the curved edges taut while serging to prevent them from curling.

No rule in our books says a facing has to be on the inside, especially when it becomes the focal point of the garment! Pati and Karen applied their facings to the outside of their jackets for the look of a separate band.

NOTE: Use this technique on unlined jackets only; lining needs to be sewn to a conventional inside facing.

Framed Facing

For Pati's band look, follow these steps:

1. Interface the facing piece. (Pati chose ArmoWeft in black so that it wouldn't show after cutting her machine buttonholes.) Then sew shoulder seams of facing and jacket.

2. Trim 4" of seam allowance away from bottom of the facing. (You'll see why in step 5.)

3. Serge bottom edges of facings, trimming off hem allowances.

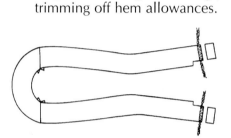

4. Serge the long unnotched edge of facing with knife just trimming edge. Tuck the chain tails from step 3 under the facing to prevent the knife from cutting them off.

5. Hem jacket, then align wrong side of facing to right side of jacket. Serge, trimming off seam allowances, and again tucking under chain tails at lower edges.

NOTE: When Pati tried Decor 6 in both loopers, she got MANY skipped stitches when serging through four layers of fabric at shoulder seams. She switched to Decor 6 in upper looper only and got fewer skipped stitches. You can repair a skipped stitch by bringing the loops together with a needle and thread.

6. Use narrow strips of fusible web to anchor loose edge of facing to jacket. (Pati tried to hand and machine stitch the edge in place, but favored the look of fusing. The web has held up during wearing and dry-cleaning.)

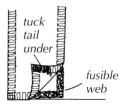

tuck tail under

fusible web

Note the self-fabric "dot" fused to the wrong side of jacket at top edge of pocket. If done before topstitching, it will reinforce pocket.

Woolly nylon was used for seams and seam finishes. Two decorative threads are used together with a longer stitch length on facing edge.

Edged Facing

Karen used the same pattern as Pati for her jacket and applied the facing to the outside, but decoratively serged only one edge for a dressier look. She combined Decor 6 with Madeira's Supertwist in the upper looper to add a little shine to the decorative serging on her wool jersey jacket.

1. Interface, then sew facing shoulder seams. Decoratively serge outer edge.

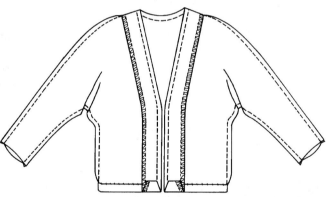

2. Sew shoulder and side seams of jacket.

3. Hem jacket.

4. Pin facing to neckline and front edges, right side of facing to WRONG side of hemmed jacket. Turn up hem of facing. Stitch facing to jacket. Trim, clip and turn facing to right side and press.

5. Topstitch facing to jacket, following NEEDLE line of serging. Tack lower edge of facing to lower edge of jacket with invisible hand stitches.

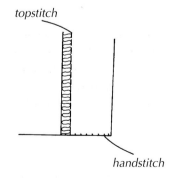

topstitch

handstitch

Yarn-Look Edgestitching

Marta's daughter, Staci, models a classic suit for school. The boiled wool jacket features yarn-look edgestitching without the bulk of yarn. How? Madeira's Burmilana provides the solution. Use two strands of it in the upper looper for a denser look, and one strand in the lower looper. Use regular thread in the needle.

1. Place facing on the jacket, wrong sides together. Machine baste on 5/8" seam line.

2. Serge, trimming off the entire seam allowance, using the stitching line as a guide for the knife.

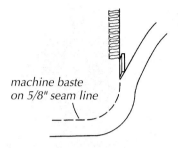

machine baste on 5/8" seam line

SPECIAL TIP: To mix two threads in the upper looper when you don't have an extra spool rod, place one spool on the table behind your machine. Make sure the threads are separated as they go through the first thread guide. Check constantly for tangles (more prevalent when using two different threads).

Of course, Marta made the pleated skirt and crisp white blouse to coordinate. The blouse's special decorative stitching (with a conventional machine) lends a custom, European touch to the entire ensemble! Similar decorative stitching has been done on Pati's blouse, too.

Casual Flatlocked Jacket

By choosing to accent her jacket with flatlocking, Lynn was able to "kill two birds with one stone." Flatlock topstitching along the front of the jacket is not only decorative, but it also provided a line on which to anchor the facing with straight stitching.

To unify the look, Lynn added flatlock topstitching to the collar as well, and flatlocked the shoulder seams. The shine of the tan rayon thread (40 wt.) in the upper looper provides a subtle contrast to the matte white cotton sweatshirt fleece; but Lynn cautions that the slippery thread pulls easily, a consideration when durability is important.

1. Before beginning to construct the jacket, lay front facing piece on jacket front and draw a fold line with vanishing marker along the inside edge of the facing. Set facing aside.

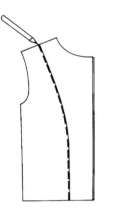

2. Flatlock along the folds, wrong sides together.

> **SPECIAL TIP**: You'll need to serge one front from top to bottom and other from bottom to top for stitches to look the same on both sides.

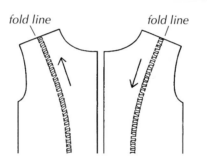

3. Fold upper collar, wrong sides together, on a line parallel with and 1" away from the collar seam line; flatlock on the fold. Pull flat.

4. Fold each end of upper collar, on a line parallel with the end seams; flatlock on the fold, crossing first row of flatlocking. Pull flat. Construct collar as usual.

5. Flatlock shoulder seams, wrong sides together.

6. Complete construction of jacket as pattern directs.

7. From right side, straight stitch along inner edge of flatlocking, anchoring facing in place.

> NOTE: Lynn embellished the back with flatlocking on the fold and created the look of a yoke and seams. She also flatlocked the sleeve on the fold from placket opening up to simulated yoke seam.

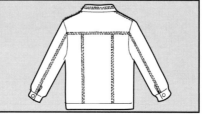

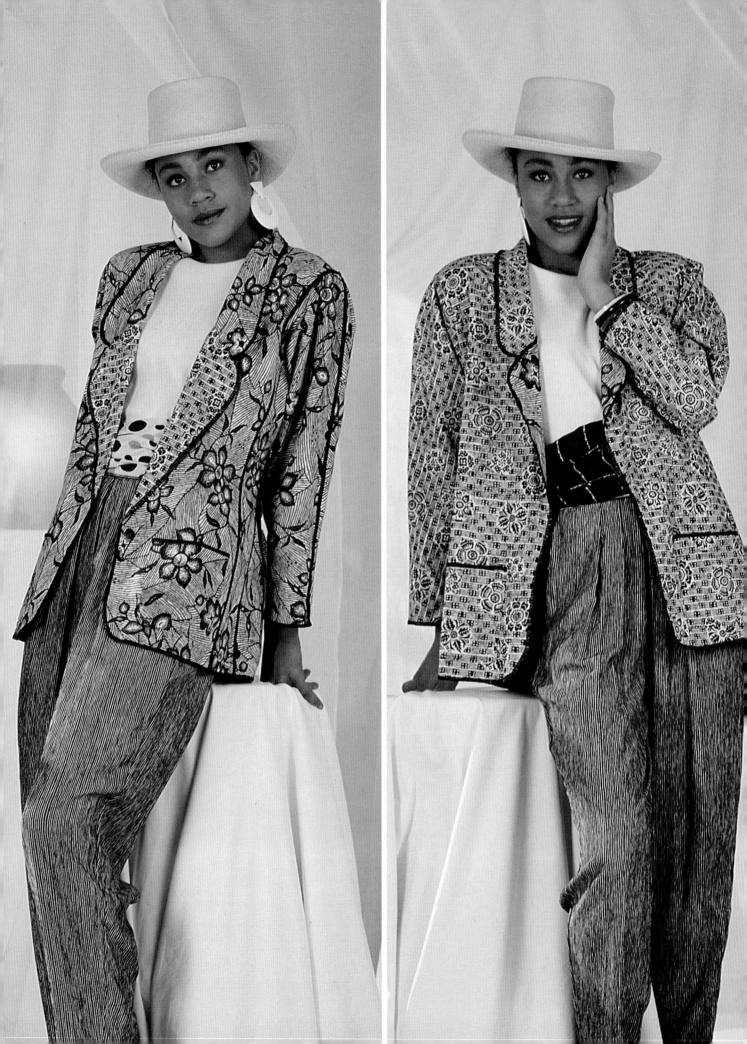

REVERSIBLE BATIK JACKET

Marta had fun with two different patterns of batik to make her "4-step" jacket completely reversible. That meant the pattern she chose had to have a cut-on sleeve. She cut the pattern out of both fabrics, placed them wrong sides together and treated them as one.

Marta used pearl cotton #8 in the upper looper and topstitching thread in the lower looper. But she says if she had to do it over again, she would choose her thread so that both could be the same, because the difference is detectable where the lapel turns back.

1. Fold pocket facings to wrong side and serge along the fold. Turn under other edges and topstitch pockets in place on jacket fronts.

2. Baste jacket pieces, cut from each fabric, wrong sides together.

3. Serge jacket seams together, through all four layers, with a balanced 3-thread stitch.

4. Press seams to one side and topstitch.

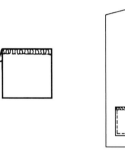 

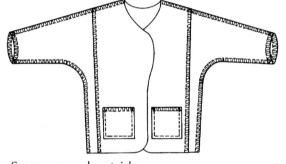

topstitch

5. Serge underarm seams. Press to one side and topstitch flat.

NOTE: Follow this serging order (fronts, backs, shoulder, bottom of sleeves, STOP!):

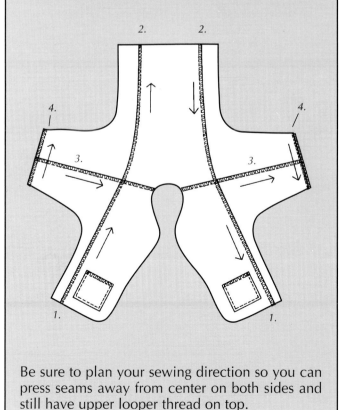

Be sure to plan your sewing direction so you can press seams away from center on both sides and still have upper looper thread on top.

6. Serge around outside edges of collars wrong sides together.

7. Machine baste collar to neckline to assure accuracy prior to serging.

8. Now serge around entire outside edges of jacket, starting at center back neck, catching collar as you go. (Collar will cover stopping point.)

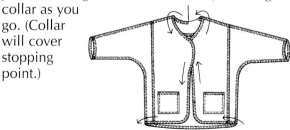

9. Serge other underarm seam. Press to one side and topstitch flat.

THE WOOL COATING STORY

We call this grouping our "wool coating story," because we have four variations on the theme of decorative outside edges, all translated in wool coating fabric. Karen, Marta and Pati made theirs from the same pattern, with slight variations—Marta rounded the collar and lapel points to avoid turning corners and Pati left the collar off entirely. Ann chose a pattern with a shawl collar—easier than a conventional collar.

We will point out the differences among the jackets, so you can be inspired to create your own using some of these ideas. All used a balanced 3-thread stitch, but note the variation in stitch length. Since coatings don't ravel, you can have a more open stitch if you wish.

FOUR JACKETS, SIX DIFFERENCES

Threads

On her pink jacket, Marta used topstitching thread AND variegated fine metallic thread *together* in the upper looper, aqua topstitching thread alone in the lower looper and aqua regular thread in the needle. She stopped and reversed stitching at the roll line, so that serging on the lapel would match that on the lower front edges.

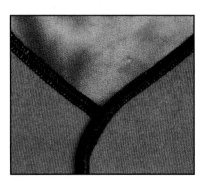

Pati used black Decor 6 rayon in the upper and lower looper and regular black thread in the needle. She found the Decor 6 wore better (didn't pill) when a longer stitch was used.

Karen used Madeira's Supertwist in white together with dark blue top-stitching thread in the lower looper and needle. Karen says she "bought out the store" of its topstitching thread—10 to 12 spools! She ended up using parts of most of them. Since the spool she used had only 50 yards, she had to plan ahead not to run out in the middle of an edge. She, like Marta, reversed stitching at the roll line (see page 114).

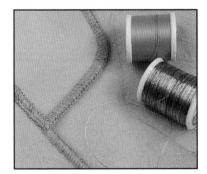

Ann decided on texturized nylon to decoratively serge her pink wool coat because it is a thread that works in both loopers of her machine. She wanted the stitch to be reversible, so that she could stitch continuously from the hem at the front, around the collar, and back down the other front.

Pockets

Note the differences in the pockets. Marta's pink with blue and Pati's fuchsia with black have the facing folded to the inside and are serged on all other edges. They were then topstitched to the jacket. Karen's yellow coating was heavy enough to eliminate the facing, so she merely serged on ALL sides of the pocket. Ann decided to flatlock topstitch across the top of the pocket, then turned down the facing and applied the pocket conventionally.

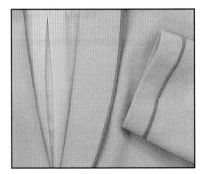

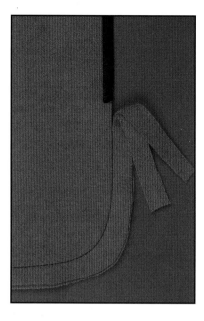

Facings:

Only Karen's yellow wool had enough body to be totally single layer. She eliminated the front facing. Pati's merino wool was so soft, she not only used the facing, but interfaced it as well. Ann did the same.

Pati suggests straight stitching your facing and jacket wrong sides together on the seam line. Then, when you serge, your knife will follow stitching, assuring the entire seam allowance is evenly trimmed away.

Outside Edge Stitching:

Karen and Marta stitched from the roll line on the right side of the front around the lower part of the jacket to the other roll line, then released the chain from the stitch finger (see page 115) and chained off. They continued sewing the lapel on the facing side around the neckline to the bottom of the roll line on the other side.

Pati and Ann did not need to do this because they used the same thread in the upper and lower looper. Ann's jacket has a square bottom, so stopping at the lower front edges was a natural.

Sleeve bottoms:

Ann accented the sleeve hems with flatlock topstitching to match the pockets. She folded each piece on a line an inch from the hem fold, set her tension dials for flatlocking, then serged along the fold. She flattened the fabric and—VOILÀ!—topstitching! She did this before sewing the sleeve seams or hemming.

Karen serged off the hem allowance on her sleeves before sewing the sleeve seam. Pati and Marta chose not to decorate their sleeves.

Collar Application:

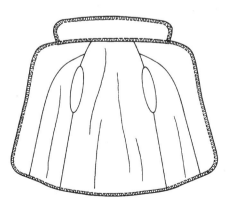

Karen and Marta stitched around ALL edges of their collars, removing the seam allowances as they serged. Then, after the jacket had been serged on all outside edges, they lapped the collar over the neckline seam and topstitched it in place on a conventional machine. Karen stitched along the INSIDE of her serging, but Marta wanted a more meshed look so topstitched along the OUTER edge of her collar serging.

Special Tips:

- Both Pati and Marta found they needed to tape the inside of the back neckline to help prevent stretch. They serged over twill tape.

- As you serge over thicker layers or around curves, be sure to guide your fabric so it doesn't get hung up under the presser foot and cause stacking of the thread (see page 28). Practice on scraps to get the "feel" of your fabric.

- Thicker layers require looser looper tensions. Thinner layers require tighter looper tensions. Practice on scraps going from thick to thin to thick to see what you need to do before serging your actual jacket. This is important when going from double layer faced fronts to single layer hem edges.

- If you use differential feed set on 2 to prevent stretch around curves, you may need to increase the stitch length a bit at the same time.

- Unless upper and lower looper threads are identical you must reverse stitching on lapel to keep decorative stitching on top. Start and stop at the bottom of the roll line:

1. Where you reverse stitching at the lapel, be sure to begin and end with an unchained tail. Pull with finger to loosen needle thread to release stitches from stitch finger.

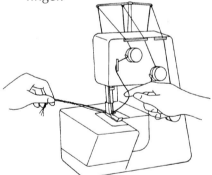

2. Stitch lower jacket from roll line to roll line with right side of the fabric on top.

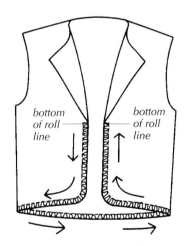

3. Then stitch from facing side, roll line to roll line.

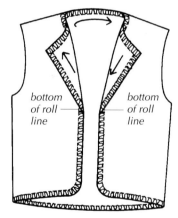

4. When you join previous stitching, overlap two stitches.

> Note: This is the same technique we use for repairing "hiccups" shown on page 35 of our book, **Creative Serging**.

5. When stitching is completed, pull all threads to wrong side. Knot. Dab knots with a seam sealant like Fray Check® or Fray-No-More®. Trim or bury threads in seam.

REVERSIBLE DOUBLE-WOVEN WOOLS

Double cloth is made of two fabrics woven one above the other and joined at the center with threads. Its reversibility, ravel resistance and sturdy quality make it ideal for single-layer construction methods, inspiring Lynn to create her short jacket.

To make the jacket completely reversible, Lynn selected a pattern with a cut-on sleeve and a thread that would work in both loopers. After testing, she found she could achieve the appearance of yarn from TWO STRANDS of Burmilana acrylic thread in each looper. Rather than buy four spools, however, Lynn wound thread onto bobbins and placed them on the serger's spool pins. She set the stitch width on the maximum setting (6 mm on her machine).

1. Trim entire hem allowance off sleeves.

2. Serge shoulder and side seam allowances, trimming off 3/8" at the same time, so that the needle traces the seam line.

3. Lap shoulder seams, aligning needle threads. Topstitch on the needle line, through both layers, then tuck under shoulder seam tail chains and serge off bottom sleeves.

4. Lap one side seam, aligning needle threads. Topstitch on the needle line, through both layers.

5. Starting at open side seam, continuously serge fronts, neck and hem over cording (page 23) to stabilize the outer edges, which are mostly curved.

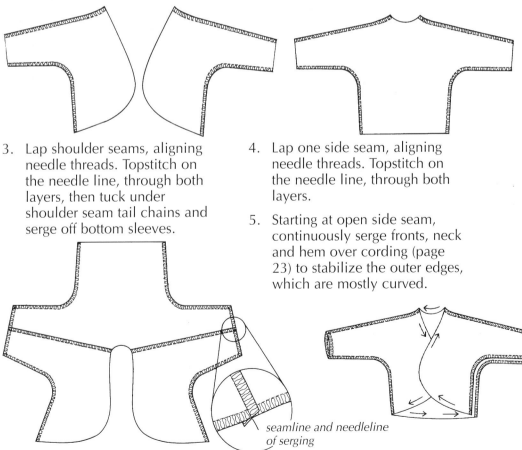

seamline and needleline of serging

6. Lap other side seam, aligning needle threads. Topstitch on the needle line, through both layers.

FOUR-STEP
JACKETS

Tapestry fabric is not always reversible, but when it is, it makes an ideal choice for SINGLE-LAYER construction methods. Where the lapel turns back, the reverse side of the fabric shows, revealing a variation of the woven design.

Marta simply followed her four-step jacket method. She used Decor 6 in both loopers so she didn't need to reverse stitches at the roll line.

1. Serge lower edge of sleeve, then sew sleeve seam.

2. Fold down pocket facing. Serge edge of pocket. Topstitch pockets onto jacket.

3. Stitch one side seam. Serge around jacket. (There's no need to reverse direction at lapel if you use the same thread in both loopers as Marta did.) Serge around collar.

4. Lap collar onto neckline and topstitch.

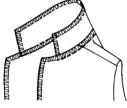

Polar Fleece Is Perfect

Polar fleece makes an ideal beginning serger project—and a great child's coat. It is ravel resistant and thick, making it ideal for single-layer construction. Pati used variegated cotton crochet thread in the upper looper and regular thread in the lower looper and needle.

1. Serge the lower edge of sleeves, outer edge of collar (single layer), and pockets.

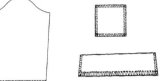

2. Topstitch pockets in place, catching outer edge of serged loops. Sew shoulder and side seams of coat using a balanced 3-thread stitch. Sew sleeve seams and set into armholes.

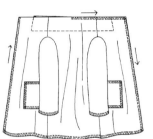

3. Stitch outer edges of coat catching collar as you go.

> **SPECIAL TIP:** You may find it easier to first machine baste collar to neckline.

4. Make coordinating buttons. Serge both sides of small triangles. Roll into a cylinder, tuck under tails, and hand stitch to hold. Sew onto coat.

NOTE: This coat is a great place to practice turning corners. (Better than serging off the edge with heavier threads.) The top and bottom of the front and one side of the top of each pocket have corners that will need turning.

1. Pretrim 2-3" of seam allowance next to corner before serging. Serge one edge to the corner.

1 stitch over the edge

2-3"

2. Pull slack in needle thread and slip corner off stitch finger (see page 115).

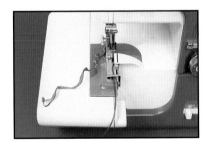

> **SPECIAL TIP:** Do a test sample with three colors of thread. If you have a loop at your corner, check the color and pull up just above tension dial to tighten that thread after turning next corner.

3. Turn fabric and insert needle close to top edge and same distance from edge as needle was from other edge.

needle position

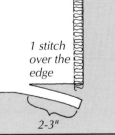

> **SPECIAL TIP:** Lower needle into fabric BEFORE lowering feed dogs.

Jackets
WITH INSIDE DECORATIVE SERGING

Not quite ready for decorative serging on the outside of your garment? Have fun with it on the inside! Many of us with Palmer/Pletsch have been individualizing the insides of jackets for years with custom piping where lining meets facing, or with conventional machine scallop stitching on the facing edge of an unlined jacket. Now we can add decorative serging to the list of special touches.

Lynn's and Karen's jackets illustrate three different techniques for decoratively serging the inside of a lined jacket:

- Flatlocking edge of facing then attaching lining.

- Flatlocking facing and lining together.

- Serging over ribbon and hand stitching it onto facing next to lining as a "braid" embellishment.

Flatlocked Facings Plus Lining

Lynn serged the facing before attaching the lining to her brown wool tweed and black linen jackets in the following manner:

1. Fold under the 5/8" seam allowance on unnotched edge of facing. Flatlock on the fold with seam allowance DOWN, so that the stitch will be entirely to the facing side of the seam line. (Lynn used Candlelight metallic yarn in the tweed jacket, while the linen features rayon thread together with Madeira's "sparkley" Supertwist, all in the upper looper.)

2. Pull flat.

3. Straight stitch lining to facing, very close to row of flatlocking (or slip stitch by hand).

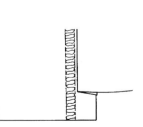

> NOTE: For complete instructions on lining jackets and coats, see our book **Easy, Easier, Easiest Tailoring** by Pati Palmer and Susan Pletsch.

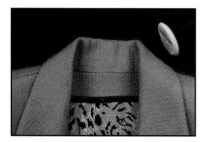

Flatlocking Lining to Facing

For her camel herringbone jacket, Karen flatlocked lining to facing with Decor 6 in the upper looper (2 mm stitch length), completing a seam and achieving a decorative look at the same time! Then she sewed the lining/facing unit to the outside edges of the jacket using the "quick lining" technique from *Easy, Easier, Easiest Tailoring*, page 188.

1. Sew jacket and lining seams. Set in sleeves on each. Press up hem allowance on lower edge of lining. Press under front edge seam allowances of lining.

2. Sew front and back neck facings together at shoulder seams. Attach collar. Trim away facing seam allowances as shown.

press under seam allowance   *turn up hem*

3. Place facing and folded lining edges WRONG sides together with facing up; flatlock without trimming folds to bottom edge of facing.

4. Pull seam flat. You will see loops on the facing next to the lining.

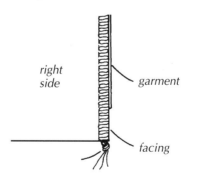

right side   *garment*

facing

5. Sew facing/lining unit to jacket. Finish lower edge of facing and "jump hem" lining (see *Easy, Easier, Easiest Tailoring*).

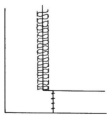

Custom Serger Braid Trim

To embellish her peach basket-weave jacket, Lynn created her own braid trim:

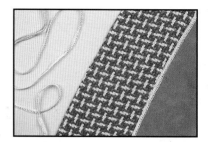

1. Serge over 1/8" satin ribbon with a narrow balanced 3-thread stitch with a width of 2.5 mm and a length of 3 mm. Lynn used Decor 6 in the upper looper. She guided the ribbon between the needle and the knife while serging. (If your machine has a tape guide on the foot, use it, or an elastic applicator foot without the tension screw tightened, here. Also see pages 23 and 119 for how to feed ribbon.)

2. Glue the "braid" on top of the facing/lining seam with Sobo glue. (It could be hand-tacked in place, but the glue holds well and is faster—but use it sparingly so it doesn't go through to the right side—it's permanent!)

SPECIAL TIP: Use this technique to personalize ready-to-wear jackets as well as those you sew.

More Decoratively Serged Lining Ideas...

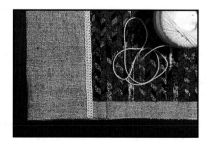

A Glenn plaid with lining stitched next to flatlocked facing. Thread: Decor 6 rayon

Ultrasuede with lining stitched next to flatlocked facing. Thread: Candlelight metallic yarn

Boiled wool with print lining stitched next to flatlocked facing. Thread: Decor 6 rayon

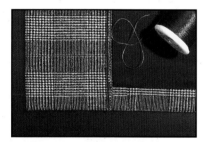

Raw silk with print lining stitched next to flatlocked facing. Thread: Pearl cotton #5

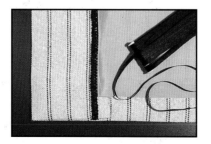

Striped linen with lining stitched next to flatlocked facing. Thread: Silk ribbon

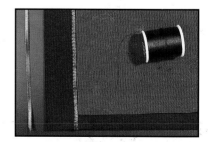

With topstitching thread in your looper, stitch over 1/8" ribbon with a long stitch length. Topstitch ribbon next to lining through facing only.

123

Pretty Unlined Jackets—Seam Finish Ideas

Before sergers, we had always recommended lining jackets because it's faster than finishing all those seam allowances with the conventional machine, and it covers the inner construction to make the inside look as professional as the outside. But with the serger, seam allowances can be finished very fast AND professionally. Now we have a choice, depending on the fabric and style of the garment. Fitted jackets should be lined, but loose-fitting ones can be left unlined or lined in the sleeves only.

The times that you elect to leave a garment unlined, why not have some fun with the serged edge finish, and individualize it at the same time? You can choose among a host of specialty threads to express yourself with flair—on the inside—even when you must be coolly conservative on the outside.

Pati's black linen and Marta's green wool tweed are fine examples. Variegated pearl cotton #5 was Pati's choice, while Marta serged with black Woolly Nylon. After shortening the stitch length, the result resembles the couture look of a Hong Kong seam finish.

More Ideas for Decoratively Serged Unlined Jackets

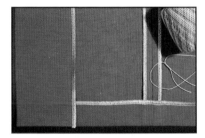

Even though seams don't need finishing in a doubleknit, it adds a decorative touch to an unlined jacket.
Thread:Variegated crochet thread

Linen is great for oversized jackets.
Thread: Heavy twisted rayon

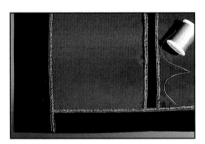

Black velvet adorned with gold.
Thread: Metallic thread

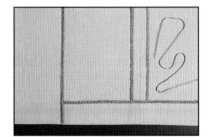

Add life to grey linen with bright fuchsia.
Thread: Silk ribbon

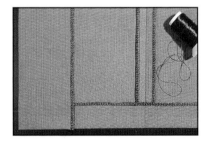

Aqua linen with its color complement, red-orange.
Thread: Shiny heavy acrylic

A pink jacquard suiting with a hint of gold picked up by the gold seam finishing.
Thread: Medium metallic

Creative Kids

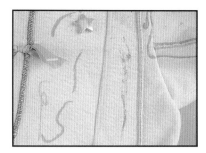

Flatlocked and Painted Sweatshirt Dresses

Sweatshirt fabrics are ideal for kids. They're easy to sew, easy care, and inexpensive. In fact, you can often purchase bolt ends or remnants to make an entire outfit for just a few dollars.

A sweatshirt DRESS similar to these Pati made for her daughter Melissa and her friend Kelsey would make an ideal first project for motivating kids to sew. It requires virtually no fitting, is easy to sew, and gives kids a chance to express their creativity with puff paints.

After cutting out the pieces of fleece, Pati added the random flatlock topstitching in several colors and types of thread: fine rayon, fine metallic and texturized nylon. Where a "hiccup" occurred, she cleverly covered it with a ribbon bow, then added a few more for good measure. After constructing the sweatshirt, Pati really went wild and decorated it more with glitter, puff paints, and sew-on stars. It's a project that's sure to bring out the kid in all of us!

Boy's "Ladderized" Sweatsuit

Testing can yield unexpected conclusions. When Lynn tested flatlock serging on this two-tone child's sweatshirt, she was surprised to discover that she didn't like the "loops" out, the look she usually wants when flatlocking for decorative effect. She found she did like "ladders" out, however, so that is the method she followed to construct every seam of the sweatshirt—even the ribbings. All threads are texturized nylon.

Special Tip: Through the course of sewing and wearing a number of flatlocked garments, we've found a seam crossed with another seam often pulls apart—because the thread tail is cut off one seam when crossed by another. Here's how to prevent little "holes" where a seam intersects the flatlocking:

flatlocking

seam

hole

1. Before sewing a seam, pretrim 1-2" of the seam allowance to be crossed, the width of what the knife would be cutting.

2. Flatlock your seam.

3. Pull seam flat and tuck tail under the edge. Sew the second seam, but **DO _NOT_** cut the tail of the first seam. (PRETRIMMING MAKES THIS POSSIBLE!)

tail tucked under (or weave in with tapestry needle)

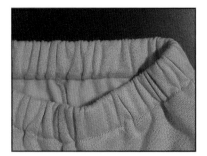

Lynn serged matching sweatpants with balanced 3-thread seams using texturized nylon for strength. A flatlocked casing holds the elastic.

1. Fold casing to inside, then fold it back on itself, keeping fold and raw edge even like a flatlock hem. Flatlock close to the fold.

2. Pull flat. Insert elastic through a hole left in the center back seam.

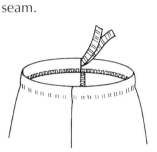

A Christmas Sweatshirt

The Christmas sweatshirt is Karen's expression of holiday cheer with its unique "wreath" yoke. To create the familiar "sectioned" appearance on the wreath, Karen flatlocked ribbon in place.

1. Serge the lower edge of front and back "wreath" pieces with a 3-thread narrow (2.5 mm) stitch width and satin (.5 mm) stitch length using YLI's "Christmas color" variegated Woolly Nylon in the upper looper. Regular serger thread in red in the lower looper and needle "frames" the stitch.

2. Flatlock on the fold over ribbon to create the "wreath sections." Use a long stitch length and matching thread in order to see the shiny satin ribbon. Hand tack ribbon tail to under side of wreath yoke.

3. Serge one shoulder seam, catching yoke front and back in seam.

4. Attach neckline ribbing wrong sides together with ribbing on top.

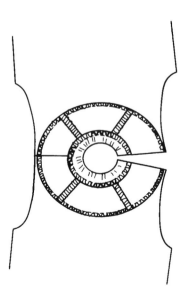

5. Topstitch neck ribbing seam down

topstitching

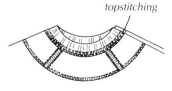

6. Roll edge top of ribbing so that it lettuces.

7. Sew other shoulder seam and set in the sleeves.

NOTE: Make sure neck opening will fit over head, as the woven wreath fabric does not allow it to stretch.

8. Attach cuff ribbing wrong sides together. The seam will slightly "lettuce."

9. Sew one underarm and sleeve seam. Attach lower ribbing wrong sides together. The seam will slightly "lettuce."

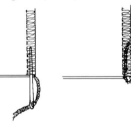

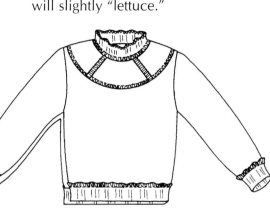

10. Sew other underarm seam. Bury thread tails in seams using a tapestry needle.

11. Attach plastic candy canes, or, for a whimsical note, you can attach REAL candy canes— they won't last long, of course!

NOTE: Karen did not topstitch sleeve and lower band ribbing down. She liked the "floppy" look of the slightly lettuced seams.

Thread Sampler Sweatshirt

Karen created this fanciful sweatshirt in order to have a "thread sampler" as a teaching tool. Six different choices adorn the "yoke." To avoid flatlocking in a circle, Karen left one back raglan seam open.

Karen marked the placement line for each row with vanishing marker. After folding on the line, wrong sides together, she flatlocked along the fold with stitches hanging slightly off the edge.

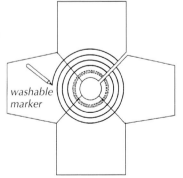

washable marker

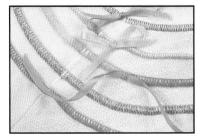

Karen recommends serging with the upper bodice edge up and the lower bodice side down against the throat plate. That way, if a slight ridge forms when you flatten the stitch, the ridge will be toward the bottom of the sweatshirt. It is important to be consistent throughout the garment.

The ribbing was attached by flatlocking, wrong sides together, with ribbing up, using texturized nylon in the upper looper.

Feminine Fleece

Sweatshirt fleece need not be limited to sweatshirts, as Lynn's dress for Melissa portrays. The color and print, the pattern choice and the lettuce edging all contribute to a very feminine look indeed!

Lynn wanted to use texturized nylon thread to do the lettuce, but couldn't find an exact color match. Through testing she found that TWO DIFFERENT shades of pink used together in the looper of the 2-THREAD rolled edge would yield a soft heather look to coordinate beautifully with the print. In addition, the double strand covered the edge better, especially on the white ribbing.

Since ribbing has "ribs," the rolled edge (and thus lettuce) is more attractive if serged over a folded edge—and so the ribbings of this dress are double layer, while the hem edge is "lettuced" on the single layer. Lynn found the differential feed feature set at 0.7 helped s-t-r-e-t-c-h the fabric as she serged.

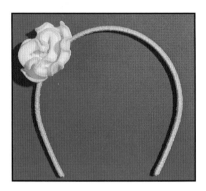

Palmer/Pletsch always stresses the importance of accessorizing, and this child's dress is no exception! Lynn wrapped a plain plastic headband with rolled edge chain to create a custom hair ornament. It meant she had to generate LOTS of chain, but the machine did the work!

Lynn guided the chain off the stitch finger to produce a taut, not loopy, strand. Then she wrapped the headband, gluing with Sobo Glue as she wrapped.

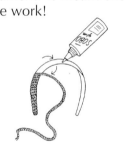

The serged rosette contributes the ultimate finishing touch. Fold in half lengthwise a 10" x 2" strip of ribbing. Roll edge the fold and gather the other edge. Roll into a rosette. Hand sew to hold in place and to anchor to headband.

An Easy Peter Pan Collar

The red corduroy jumper and coordinating blouse also involved pattern modification. Double-layer ruffles, as specified for the jumper, would have been too bulky for corduroy, so Lynn cut them single thickness, and finished their edges with Woolly Nylon in the upper looper.

She edged the blouse's ruffles in the same way, and applied the collar to the wong side of the neckline using the quick Peter Pan collar technique. As the photo at right shows, the seam is hidden under the collar (see our book **Sewing With Sergers**, page 72).

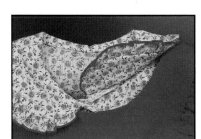

Color-Blocked Cotton Playsuit

If a day on the beach is the plan, Staci is all set to go in her two-piece play suit, made in a flash on the serger. Marta combined serger and conventional machine techniques to whip up the two-tone, pull-on "jams" shorts. Edges of the buttoned top were finished with the rolled edge stitch (pearl cotton #8 in the upper looper), eliminating all the trimming, turning and pressing required for conventional faced edges.

Marta even added serged pintucks to the pocket for a coordinating touch.

1. Self-interface pocket by cutting on an additional facing width. Serge finish top edge with balanced 3-thread stitch.

2. Press under "interfacing."

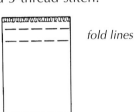

fold lines

3. Serge outer edges of pocket with rolled edge.

4. Serge rolled edge "tucks."

5. Press down facing.

6. Topstitch pocket to top.

Rolled Edge Hair Bow

Marta made a matching hair bow to accessorize as follows:

1. Roll edge serge, wrong sides together, the outer edges of two strips of fabric 20" long and 1 3/4" wide, trimming off 1/8". Do the same for a strip 3" long and 1 3/4" wide.

2. Fold long strip into double bow.

3. Wrap center with short strip. Hand stitch in place.

4. Sew to a barrette.

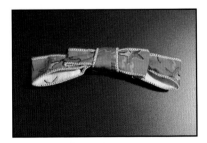

Decorative Overalls

Pati made the green cotton playsuit for Melissa and was delighted to experience the ease of flat construction methods.

Small enclosed areas, such as the bib, straps, and pocket are never any fun to trim, turn and press; but decorative serging can eliminate much of that. You simply place the two layers wrong sides together, then serge around. Pati used texturized nylon in both loopers and the needle. After serging the bib, Pati topstitched it to the pants by straight stitching along the serging.

Some tips to make this type of child's garment easy:

- Use texturized nylon for durability and for good coverage. Use a "thread cradle" to help get it through the loopers and needle (see page 27).

- Pati used about a 1 mm stitch length. (A shorter length covers better, but it may cause stretching on the bias edges and curves. If so, try lengthening a bit.)

- Use a press cloth to press over texturized nylon thread. Too hot an iron can melt it.

- Serge each edge of bib, straps and pocket (all double thickness).

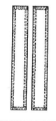

inside corner

NOTE: See page 68 for turning inside corners on a serger.

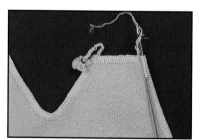

- Pull tails through serging using a loop turner (photo) or a tapestry needle (see page 129).

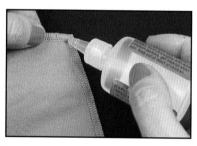

- Cut off excess tails. Dot seam sealant (Fray Check® or Fray No More™) on wrong side of corners to reinforce. Let dry 5 minutes.

Baby's Quilted Overalls

Kelsey is ready for action in creative overalls! While Lynn chose to "wrap" the edges with texturized nylon in the upper looper (see page 148), she found she got more "pokeys" with that method. She now recommends a balanced stitch (1 mm stitch length) with texturized nylon in **both** loopers. In addition, she advises that the front tab is hard to stitch around unless the curve is at least the diameter of a coffee mug.

SPECIAL TIP: Zig-zag around the edges just inside the cutting line to compress them before serging. It makes pucker-free serging easier on some quilted fabrics. Experiment.

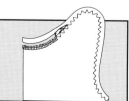

Because Lynn felt the quilted cotton's tricot backing would not be durable, or comfortable next to the skin, she backed it with a coordinating print fabric. She cut two of each piece, placed wrong sides together, then treated them as one with decorative seaming on the outside. The overalls aren't reversible because the grippers only work one way. Besides, the inside isn't as much "fun" without contrasting seaming.

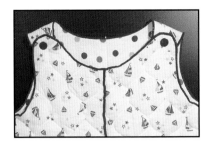

A "Daisy Kingdom" Special

Temptation abounds at the Daisy Kingdom in Portland, Oregon—the most unusual fabric store in North America. Their manufacturing division designs fabrics like that found in the collar of this dress that Lynette Black, Palmer/Pletsch promotions manager, made for her daughter Kelsey.

Lynette put Decor 6 in her upper looper and roll edged the entire single layer bib collar, running enough chain off the edge at the center back neck to bring it back into a button loop. She says that when you roll edge on the bias, you get a few pokeys, but not enough to make her do it differently.

The coordinating calico dress was sewn together with a 3/4-thread stitch. The second needle thread gave added durability. The ruffle, bottom of sleeves and outer edges of collar were also roll edged. Lynette was going to simply sew on a ruffle, but decided that it would be more interesting to roll edge both edges of the ruffle and gather between them. (The original pattern did not have a lower ruffle at all—a CREATIVE addition!)

Heirloom Serging

In Years Past...

The art of French hand sewing originally required hours and hours of painstaking sewing, because, as the name implies, it was worked by hand. But it was a way for Victorian-era seamstresses to embellish otherwise plain fabrics. After all, they didn't have the myriad choices of prints and textures we have today.

In the past decade, the art has been revived, thanks to adaptations which permit the use of the sewing machine. Garments that used to take days, can now be done in hours, first on the conventional sewing machine and now.....

....enter the serger. The rolled edge does "rolling and whipping" twice as fast as the conventional machine AND sews a seam at the same time. The serger knives eliminate many trimming steps. The result? Garments that used to take hours, now take minutes! For complete instructions, see our book **Creative Serging**, Chapter 10.

Linda's grandmother Gladys Usher (née Wellar) poses in 1914 in her sixth grade commencement dress embellished with true French Hand Sewing.

Today In Contrast...

Staci is the picture of femininity in her two-piece heirloom dress. We could almost call this an "heirloom serging sampler" because it shows so many techniques...pintucks, lace insertion, ribbon eyelet insertion, lace trim and smocking...at waist and hipline.

Whenever pintucks and lace insertions are added, it is best to embellish the fabric before cutting out the garment. In this case Marta embellished a fabric panel before cutting out the top.

Texturized nylon was used in the upper looper for the rolled edge stitch. Its excellent coverage and durability make it ideal for serging calicos such as this. In addition to creating the heirloom effects, the rolled edge was used to hem the ruffles.

Marta began embellishing with the lace insertion in the center, then worked back and forth from one side to the other adding pintucks. (Don't build ALL of one side, then try to repeat it on the other side.)

Pay attention to sewing direction to ensure the right side of the rolled edge is the one that shows when the "roll" is pressed to one side. In other words, serge from top to bottom on one side and bottom to top on the other.

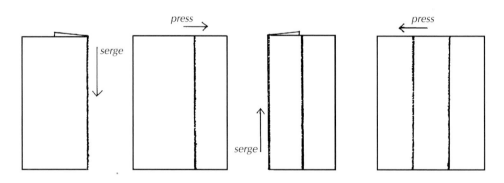

For a flatter application of the lace to the apron edges, Marta switched her tensions to flatlocking and serged lace to fabric with wrong sides together (loops out).

Flatlocking with ladders out was the basis of the smocking on the top of the skirt. Marta followed the same methods used by Karen on her wool jersey skirt (see p.62).

A Pinafore Dress

Kelsey's dot dress with pinafore exemplifies many more of the ways that the rolled edge is great for frills. Lynn used it not only to finish the ruffle, sash and hem edges; but also to attach the lace around the edges of the pinafore and to sew the pintucks. She used the conventional machine, however, to add the decorative stitches between the pintucks and to hem the sleeves. (Lynn had found after "rolling" the hem of the dress itself that the stiff dot didn't roll well. She covered that unattractive roll hem with lace trim.)

To further take advantage of the serger's speed, Lynn strayed from the pattern's instructions and attached the collar with the quick Peter Pan method (see photo on page 131 and our book **Sewing With Sergers**, p. 72).

An Heirloom Christening Dress

The ultimate heirloom project is a handsewn Christening dress for a newborn baby. But if you don't have time to do it totally by hand, let the serger assist you. Marta focused her heirloom serging on the pinafore.

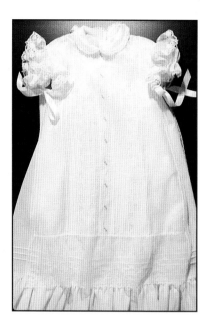

The dress fabric is a poly/cotton batiste, for durability, and the pinafore a Swiss cotton batiste, the fabric used for true French hand sewing. Marta says you'll get less puckering between rows on the Swiss cotton. However, she was pleasantly surprised at so few puckers between the rows of rolled edge pintucks on the poly/cotton batiste dress, possibly because they were done on the crosswise grain.

SPECIAL TIP: Create heirloom "yardage" before cutting out garment—it's much easier to work with!

She used the four trims shown in the photo: a wide pre-embroidered trim for a "touch" of color, entredeaux (premade embroidered strip with "hemstitched" holes down the center), insertion lace and 1" lace edging (which Marta narrowed). See our book **Creative Serging** for a complete list of lace possibilities.

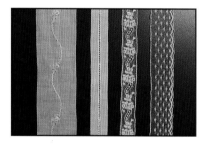

Serge the trim and entredeaux right sides together with a narrow BALANCED stitch. Serge the pin tucks in batiste and add insertion lace using a rolled edge with stitch length of 2 mm. (The longer stitch length is actually stronger and puckers less.) With a narrow balanced stitch, attach wide lace to lower edge right sides together. Lastly, serge the lace edging to the sides, finishing off the lace trim used at the lower edge at the same time.

The neckline of the pinafore was finished by serging on a bias strip of cotton batiste folded in half.

bias strip

The collar is attached using the quick Peter Pan technique (see page 131). The dress hem is sewn using the scalloped rolled edge—a simple but elegant finish.

A Beautiful Beginner's Project

A pillow is a natural first project if you're wanting to try your hand at heirloom serging. You probably won't think a pillow has to be as "perfect" as something you wear, and the "country romantic" look of such a pillow is popular today for many decorating schemes. Marta made hers all in white. With Decor 6 thread in the upper looper, she used the rolled edge to sew the pintucks and to insert the laces. She continued to use the rolled edge with Decor 6 to make serger piping (with yarn as the filler cord) to insert between the ruffle and the pillow itself. The stitch length was set at 3 mm. (If shorter than that for the rolled edge, the thread begins to fray.)

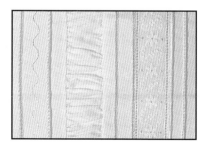

Then Marta wound the same thread onto a bobbin to sew a conventional machine serpentine stitch between pintucks and on the ruffle. Because the bobbin carries the specialty thread, the decorative stitch must be sewn with wrong side of fabric up.

Simply Elegant Suit Blouse

Lynn created her own heirloom yardage for this "simply elegant" linen/cotton blouse. She recommends starting with a length of fabric several inches longer than the pattern piece from which it will be cut, to allow for the inevitable unevenness at the ends that results from inserting laces in the fabric. Because of the differing softness of the laces and the fabrics, some bubbling may form, especially on the lengthwise grain. But this just adds more of a handmade appearance! See our book **Creative Serging** for complete instructions for heirloom serging including all the possibilities.

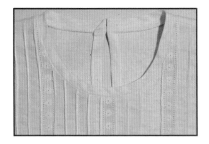

Using regular serger thread, Lynn used the rolled edge to form pintucks and to insert the laces. After testing, she found the best stitch length for this fabric and technique is 1.5 to 2 mm; otherwise, the "roll" was too bulky. She also found the tucks could not be closer together than the width of the presser foot.

Nighttime Romance

When Lynn conceived the idea of embellishing a nightgown with heirloom serging, she decided to test her scheme first on a sample piece of the charmeuse she planned to use. She was so satisfied with her test effort that she OVERLAID it on the bodice, rather than take the risk that serging directly on the garment wouldn't turn out! She chose fine rayon thread for its sheen.

Cut on the center line of the inset piece and insert a strip of lace. After adding two rows of pintucks on either side, topstitch the piece to the bodice. Join the lace to the neckline and ruffle edges with rolled-edge seaming. To form the rolled seam on the right side of the garment, start with wrong sides together.

Two Color Heirloom Nightgown

Karen was also inspired to make a nightgown to showcase her venture into heirloom serging. Using traditional batiste, Karen blended the palest blue with pure white to create a vision of softness and femininity.

With texturized nylon in the upper looper, Karen used the rolled edge stitch for all of the embellishment techniques: pintucks and lace insertions on the yoke and along the gown's lower edge and lace edging along the neckline. The yoke also features strips of the blue batiste which were inserted with the rolled edge. Finally, the edges of the ruffles were roll hemmed before being attached to the bodice.

Serge Up Instant Accessories

Accessories can provide new life for old classics and can make a $40 outfit look like it cost $200. But they can also occupy a lot of shopping time to find just the right pieces to do the job. That's where your sewing machine and serger come in. You can get exactly what you want when you make your own accessories.

Pocket Squares

That's what Kathy did to enhance her black and yellow tweed jacket. Kathy said there's only one shade of yellow that looks good on her. Imagine trying to find that perfect hue in the style of blouse she wanted if she had to rely on ready-to-wear! Good thing she sews. Not only did she find the perfect fabric for the blouse; but by sewing, she has a matching pocket square (roll hemmed in black to coordinate with her jacket).

Fringing Shawls and Scarves

Fringing requires little more than "unweaving" the edge of a fabric, one yarn at a time; but it is a technique with so many creative possibilities. Most fabrics demand a row of stitching where fringing becomes fabric again, to prevent further raveling. Why not make that row a decorative one with your serger and a specialty thread? We call it "flatlock fringe."

Wool and rayon challis are ideal fabrics for fringed scarves and shawls. They stay in place on the body better than slippery fabrics. Liberty of London, the British purveyor of posh printed fabrics, has offered its glorious wool challis prints in 54" fringed squares for decades. They seldom have an anchoring stitch where the fringe begins, but that might only be because no one has ever shown them how! Wait till you see the effects.

Flatlocked and Fringed Scarf

Pati edged her shawl in a rich brown shade of Decor 6; and "rich" is, indeed, the effect of the shiny rayon on the matte challis. Here's how:

1. Pull a thread to mark the line where you want fringing to begin. Fold the edge under on that line. Adjust your machine for flatlocking. Beginning with an unchained tail, lower needle into folded edge at first drawn thread line. Serge along the fold with fold halfway between knife and needle.

   To turn corner, slip fabric off stitch finger carefully without pulling slack in threads.

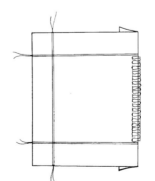
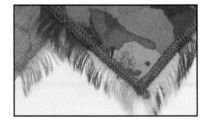

2. Open first stitching and pull flat. Fold next edge under on drawn thread line. Flatlock along fold as in step one. Repeat for all edges.

3. On the last edge, stop serging after overlapping other stitches. Remove the stitches from the stitch finger and pull fabric from machine. Tie knot in chain (page 51), and bury the tail under the stitches, using a tapestry needle (page 129).

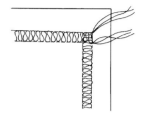

4. Pull threads out along the edges to yield fringe.

Flatlocked and Fringed Shawl

For her challis shawl, Lynn chose to fold the fabric in half diagonally before stitching because she didn't want the unattractive wrong side to show during wear. With Decor 6 rayon in the upper looper, she flatlocked through both layers before fringing.

NOTE: For more flatlock fringing see **Creative Serging**, page 58.

Flatlocked Fringed Skirt Hem

Ann immediately thought "flatlock fringed skirt" when she spotted the handsome wool check. She also thought it was an ideal place to try yarn serging. She later learned that adjusting tension for the yarn would be challenge enough, without also trying to adjust for flatlocking!

Ann chose to highlight the taupe color, allowing her to accessorize with either camel or grey. In a yarn store she found the perfect color match in a loosely-twisted yarn just thin enough to use in the serger.

Extensive testing led her to leave the yarn out of the tension disk and two thread guides, and to tighten the lower looper tension ALL THE WAY to achieve a BALANCED 3-thread stitch. (Flatlocking would have required the lower looper tension to be increased even more, but the lower looper was already as tight as it would go!) She used regular serger thread in the needle and lower looper, and sewed VERY S-L-O-W-L-Y!

1. Complete the entire skirt except for the lower edge, leaving one seam open the last several inches to avoid sewing in a circle.

2. Press hem allowance up.

3. With skirt on top (hem allowance against throat plate), decoratively serge along the fold.

4. Press hem allowance down. Topstitch serged seam over hem allowance to hold in place. Fringe hem allowance up to stitching—something to do while watching TV. Sew last seam closed.

Mini Blanket Stitch Edge Technique

The mini blanket stitch on the serger makes a speedy, soft finish for the edges of scarves as Marta's 45" oblong confirms. She used fine rayon thread in the upper looper to edge the scarf she made to wear with her aqua jacket photographed on page 102.

Set up the rolled edge on your machine. Like the regular serged blanket stitch (page 103), the needle tension must be very loose, while both looper tensions are very tight. Use a medium-long stitch length, and test until you achieve the look you like best.

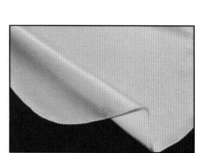

Serged Flowers

You'll recognize this rose from the cover of the book. Marta made it to accessorize her purple and silver wool jacket, purple Ultrasuede Facile skirt and silver blouse (see photo, page 38).

1. Cut a bias strip of fabric 8" x 2 1/2".

2. Roll hem one edge over fishline (see page 23 for feeding techniques), skimming the edge with the knife. Marta used regular weight rayon thread and a 2 mm stitch length.

3. Gather other edge and roll into a flower. Stitch to anchor.

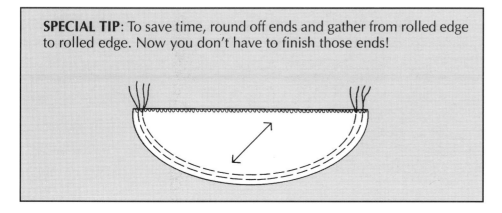

SPECIAL TIP: To save time, round off ends and gather from rolled edge to rolled edge. Now you don't have to finish those ends!

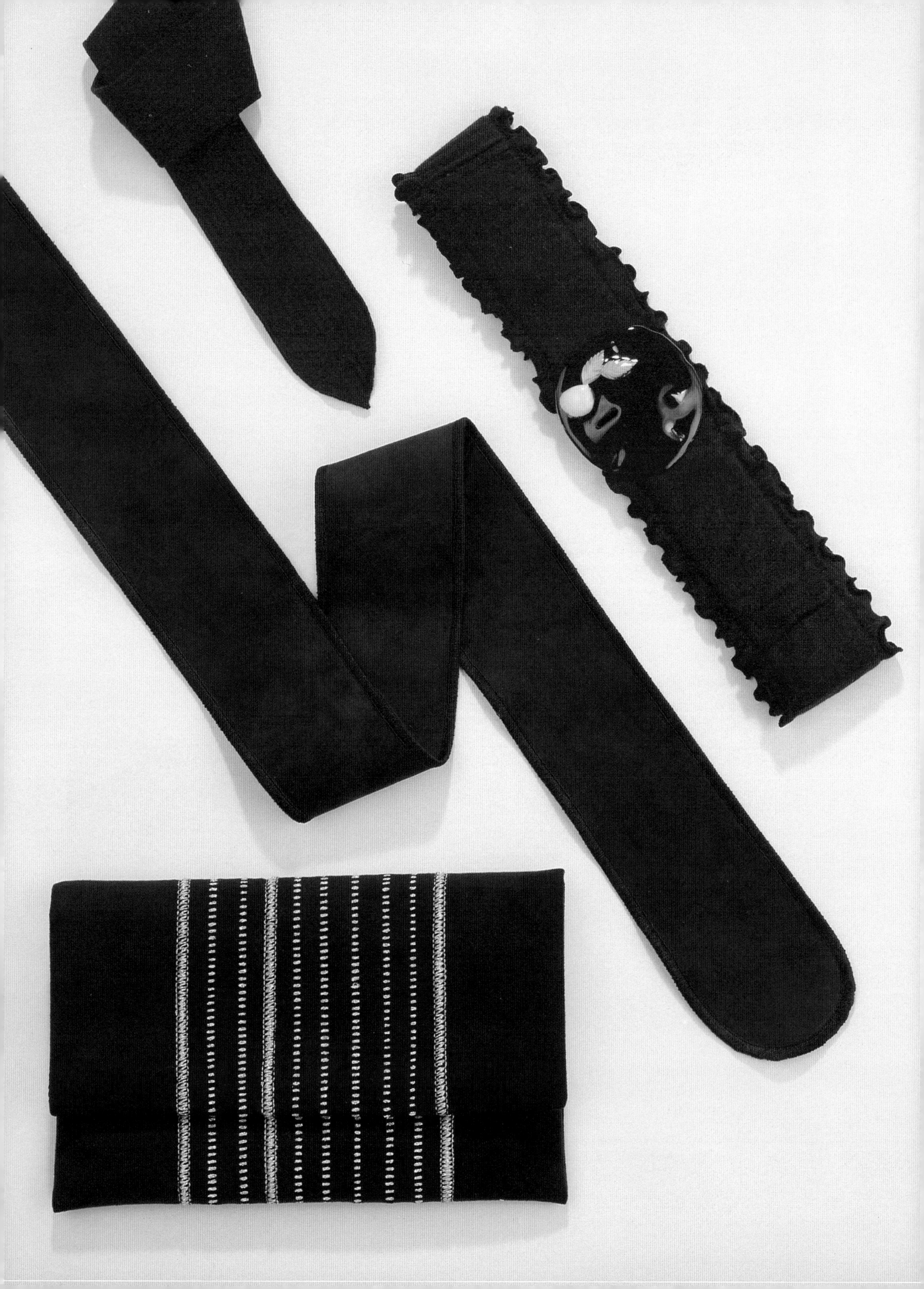

Belts and Handbags

If you have an attractive waistline, you probably delight in belts. After all, one of the principles of dressing well is to downplay your figure flaws by accentuating your assets.

The pattern companies offer a number of options when you wish to sew your own belts, and we can show you a few more to whip up in a flash on your serger. Let your imagination run wild! From plain to fancy, the possibilities are endless.

Rolled Edge Belt

One of the easiest belts is made from double faced quilted fabrics. Cut out the shape and decoratively serge the edge.

Lynn went one step further with her tie belt. She sandwiched a layer of polyester fleece between two layers of fabric 2" x 45" (one could be a contrast color) and topstitched through all layers with parallel rows of straight stitching. She then rounded the ends, and, with a balanced tension combined with the rolled edge setting, serged around the edges of the belt.

Quick Covered Belt

"Necessity is the mother of invention," as Marta can attest. She wasn't able to find the color she wanted in ready-to-wear belts; so she bought one with an interesting buckle, and covered the belt itself with her dress fabric. Here's how:

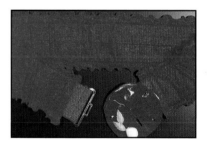

1. Cut a strip of fabric twice the width of the belting plus 2" plus seam allowances, and the length desired (Marta cut hers 6" longer than her finished belt so she'd end up with a gathered effect).

2. Seam strip on a conventional machine. Press open, turn, and center the seam.

3. Serge a lettuce rolled edge along folds. (Of course, if your fabric isn't stretchy, it won't "lettuce.")

4. Remove buckle from ready-made elastic belt. Insert that belt (or wide elastic belting) into fabric strip. Topstitch through all layers, close to both sides of the elastic.

5. Wrap belt ends around buckles and topstitch to hold.

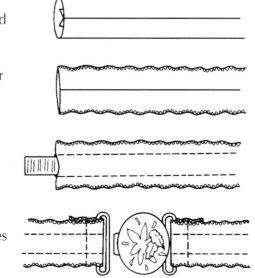

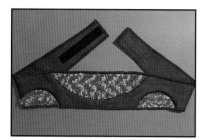

Freeform Fabric Belt

Marta made this belt to coordinate with the chambray/sweater knit top and skirt described earlier on page 94. She followed the same method, beginning by cutting the chambray to "frame" the knit in a freeform design. She serged along the edges of the chambray with pearl cotton #8, then lapped them over the knit and topstitched along both edges of the serging. Marta finished both edges of the belt with the same pearl cotton serging.

Belt With a Wrapped Edge

You may need to "wrap" an edge (upper looper thread wraps to back side) if the thread you are using works only in the upper looper and the wrong side will show, as in this tie belt. Using variegated thread makes it even more important for both sides to look the same.

Marta used two 3" x 45" pieces of Ultrasuede, fusing them together with fusible web. Rounding the ends eliminates having to serge corners. The variegated DMC pearl cotton #5 was removed from the tension disk and as many guides as possible. Texturized nylon was used in the lower looper with the tension tightened all the way. Regular thread and normal tension was used in the needle. Marta says that it is difficult to keep the upper looper thread looking perfect on the wrong side since NO tension is on it, but the finished look IS better than if a balanced stitch is used.

Decoratively Serged Ultrasuede Bag

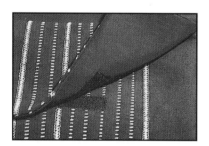

Lynn created this elegant bag from a scrap of Ultrasuede serged with Candlelight metallic yarn. Here's how:

1. Cut pieces of lining, Ultrasuede and polyester fleece 11" x 19."

2. On right side of lining sew a 2 1/2" strip of velcro 1" from one edge.

3. Flatlock parallel rows on Ultrasuede. Lynn used Candlelight in the NEEDLE for the ladders and in the UPPER LOOPER for the loops.

4. Topstitch other 2 1/2" strip of velcro 4" down from one end of Ultrasuede.

5. Fold up 6" of lining right sides together and stitch 1/4" from edge along one side and only 1" from top on other, leaving an opening in lining.

6. Pin fleece to wrong side of Ultrasuede and fold Ultrasuede right sides together. Stitch 1/4" seams through all layers.

7. Pin bag and lining flap and tops right sides together. Stitch 1/4" from edges. Clip corners. Turn through opening in lining. Topstitch opening closed.

Clever Gifts

You needn't be caught empty-handed the next time you need a gift. Just put your serger to work! Decorative serging can make even an otherwise mundane household item suitable for gift-giving. Many of these projects can be made in minutes, but your friends will exclaim, "How did you ever find the time!"

Variegated Tea Towel

Take that mundane cotton tea towel and "dress it up" with variegated serging of pearl cotton. Decoratively serge each end, then turn up and topstitch to create a hem.

Lettuce-Edge Anklets

Make a pair of little girls' anklets special with lettuce edges. Start with ready made socks; fold down rib 1", right sides together. Lettuce the fold by stretching as you serge with a rolled edge stitch, using texturized nylon for best coverage. When you fold the anklet down the lettuce will show.

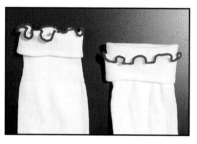

Fold down 1". Lettuce on the fold. Fold down 1" more to wear.

Child's Artist Apron

We've said it before, and Lynn's denim apron proves it again: Ideas are all around you. Lynn copied this crayon idea from a local department store. Not only is it an easy project to make for your favorite child artist, but it is also easy to turn out in minutes. Lynn used a satin stitch of texturized nylon to finish the edges.

Put the apron together as follows:

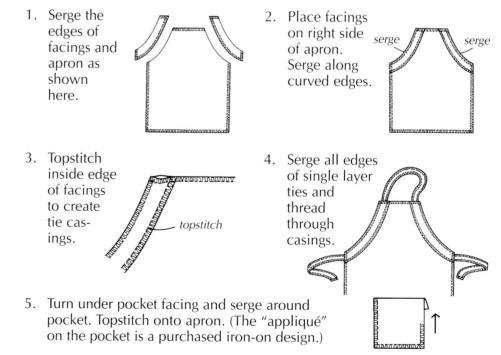

1. Serge the edges of facings and apron as shown here.

2. Place facings on right side of apron. Serge along curved edges.

   serge   *serge*

3. Topstitch inside edge of facings to create tie casings.

   topstitch

4. Serge all edges of single layer ties and thread through casings.

5. Turn under pocket facing and serge around pocket. Topstitch onto apron. (The "appliqué" on the pocket is a purchased iron-on design.)

6. Serge around crayon strip. Stitch onto apron, allowing just enough space for crayons to slip in (since crayons break easily Lynn says now she wishes she'd used washable felt-tip markers!).

Quick Home Dec Ideas

Placements and Napkins

Sewing for the home can be among the most rewarding creative pursuits. The transformation of a room from dull to dramatic yields results that can be enjoyed by the entire family every single day, and the monetary savings when you do it yourself are truly substantial. Best of all, most projects are really very simple to complete, especially when you factor in the speed of the serger.

If you're a beginner to home dec, start small with table toppings. Somehow food tastes better when it is served on a table attractively dressed with a tablecloth or placemats and cloth napkins. All are a snap to serge, and make welcome gifts.

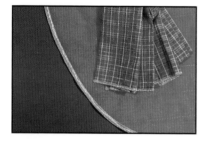

Express your creativity by coordinating interesting mixes of fabrics and textures. You can customize the table setting to your own decor or party theme—even make your own napkin rings—and have better fabrics and quality than you find among ready-mades.

Refer to our books **Sewing with Sergers**, pages 116 to 121, and **Creative Serging**, pages 115 to 119, for detailed how-to's and measurements for a variety of home dec projects. Use THIS book for full-color inspiration!

A set for the holidays is a must. Here Lynn edged red quilted cotton with gold metallic yarn in the upper looper for the placemat and napkin ring. Fine metallic thread was used in the upper looper for roll hemming the Christmas plaid napkin.

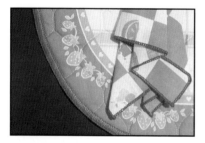

Quilted cotton prints are often available with coordinating cotton broadcloth prints, and that's what inspired Lynn to make the set here. Again, she made napkin rings to match, this time of the napkin fabric. All are edged with the same pearl cotton #5 in the upper looper; but the napkin's and ring's edges are rolled, while the placemat is finished with the balanced 3-thread stitch.

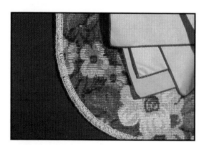

Tapestry fabric is an ideal alternative to quilted cotton for placemats. It has a suitable weight and firmness and comes in dramatic prints for when the occasion calls for something sophisticated. Lynn edged hers with metallic yarn in the upper looper. The colors of the napkin and its rolled edges (of texturized nylon) complement the mat's floral. The napkin ring is brass.

If your dishes are patterned, you may prefer the placemat to be a solid color, but that doesn't mean it has to be PLAIN. Choose a soft print for the napkin and then choose your threads accordingly. Here, the quilted cotton placemat is edged with a contrasting pearl cotton #8, while the napkin is finished with pink (also pearl cotton #8) to match the mat. The dotted ribbon around the napkin "ties" the pieces together into a coordinated look.

Those fancy catalogs filling up your mail box aren't all "junk mail." A set of table toppings in one of them inspired Marta to make a similar set and save herself the better part of the $50 price tag!

Quilt a printed fabric and a coordinating solid together, with polyester fleece sandwiched between, for your own quilted cotton placemats and table runner. Make the napkins double layer as well to cover the print's unattractive wrong side. Marta made her set of four 18" napkins and placemats and the table runner from 2 1/4 yards of each fabric.

One spool of Decor 6 thread is more than enough to edge all nine pieces. For the placemats and table runner, use a balanced 3-thread stitch set for the widest width possible and a length of about 2 mm. Leave the stitch length the same for the napkins, but use the rolled edge.

Table Topping Tips

We generally prefer the speed and ease of serging off the corners of napkins and then securing them with Fray Check. Leave the chain tails on the napkin and touch seam sealant on the corner only. Be sure it's just a tiny drop, as the sealant can alter the color of the fabric. Let the sealant completely dry, then neaten the corners with scissors.

NOTE: When using such a slippery thread as Decor 6, however, turning the corners on the serger would make them more durable to withstand many launderings.

Make placemats oval and round off corners of tablecloths to facilitate continuous serging. Use a cup or plate as a template to round off the corners. Start serging at a point that will be inconspicuous on the table in case lapping of stitches is less than perfect. On placemats use the "belly button" rule: Start serging where the mat meets your belly button (in the center of the bottom edge)! The plate will cover the joining of stitches.

When serging must begin in the middle of the edge (as on an oval placemat), start with an unchained tail. Pull lots of slack above the needle and gently pull threads out behind the presser foot, or reverse the direction of the handwheel and then pull threads out. Place fabric under foot. Serge around until you stitch over previous stitching. (Raise knife or be CAREFUL not to cut previous stitching.) Again release stitches from finger, unchain the tail and pull fabric out from under the foot.

Once you've tried your serger on table toppings, you won't hesitate to progress to larger home decorating projects. Most can be seamed and finished entirely with the serger in record time. And just think—no more tedious clipping of raveling after laundering.

A 4- or 5-thread safety stitch is ideal for seaming woven decorator fabrics. Its double chainstitch and wider seam allowance provide a secure seam, and its overedge or overlock stitch prevents raveling. If you do not have a safety stitch, and if seams will be stressed during use of the item (as might seams of a pieced quilt), sew seams first with a straight stitch, then finish edges with serging. (The seams on curtains and draperies are not subject to stress—so they may be stitched with the overlock alone.)

AFTER THE DA
SUSAN SCHELLING PHOTO

Serge A Bedroom

Dust Ruffles, Pillows and Table Skirts

Marta redecorated her daughter Staci's bedroom with the speedy help of the serger. She found a perfect match to the carpet in a collection of Waverly poly/cotton coordinates. A total of four balls of #8 DMC pearl cotton were used in the upper looper to roll edge the bed ruffle and pillow ruffles for the bed and for the skirts on the small round table. She handwound the pearl cotton onto an empty cone–and didn't get a single hiccup!

Quilted Coverlet

Before making the quilt, Marta experimented with durability. We've found that a plain 3-thread stitch is not durable enough to hold cotton pieces together in a quilt.

She seamed her six layers together with a balanced 3-thread stitch, using three balls of #8 pearl cotton in the upper looper, a 5 mm stitch width and a 2.5 mm stitch length. She then topstitched the seam down through ALL layers for GREAT durability.

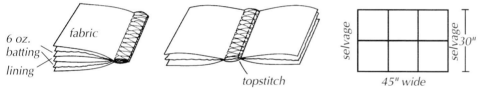

To construct the quilt:

1. Cut six 15" squares of each of the four fabric prints used (30" of each print if fabrics are 45" wide). Cut 24 squares of lining fabric and 6 oz. batting.

2. Plan your finished design as shown.

3. Sandwich fabric, batting and lining squares. Piece squares into rows according to design above. Topstitch serged seams to one side, alternating direction from strip to strip so fabric will not be too bulky to serge neatly when finishing strips.

4. With lining sides together, serge strips together. Topstitch serged strips from lining side.

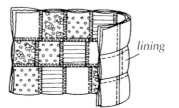

5. Decoratively serge around outside edges to finish quilt.

INDEX

PRODUCTS

These ready-to-use, information-filled sewing how-to books, manuals and videos can be found in local fabric stores or ordered through Palmer/Pletsch Publishing (see address on last page).

8½ x 11 BOOKS

☐ **The BUSINE$$ of Teaching Sewing,** *by Marcy Miller and Pati Palmer, 128 pages, $19.95* If you want to be in the BUSINESS of teaching sewing, read this book which compiles 20 years of experience of Palmer/Pletsch, plus Miller's innovative ideas. Chapters include: Appearance and Image; Getting Started; The Lesson Plan; Class Formats; Location; Marketing, Promotion & Advertising; Pricing; Teaching Techniques; and Continuing Education—Where To Find It.

☐ **Couture—The Art of Fine Sewing,** *by Roberta C. Carr, 208 pages, softcover, $29.95* How-to's of couture techniques and secrets, brought to life with illustrations and dozens of garments photographed in full color.

☐ **The Serger Idea Book—A Collection of Inspiring Ideas from Palmer/Pletsch,** *160 pgs., $19.95* Color photos and how-to's on inspiring and fashionable ideas from the Extraordinary to the Practical.

☐ **Creative Serging for the Home—And Other Quick Decorating Ideas,** *by Lynette Ranney Black and Linda Wisner, 160 pgs., $18.95* Color photos and how-to's to help you transform your home into the place YOU want it to be.

☐ **Sewing Ultrasuede® Brand Fabrics—Ultrasuede®, Ultrasuede Light™, Caress™, Ultraleather™,** *by Marta Alto, Pati Palmer and Barbara Weiland, 128 pages, $16.95* Inspiring color photo section, plus the newest techniques to master these luxurious fabrics.

Coming in early 1996:
☐ **Dream Sewing Spaces— Design and Organization for Spaces Large and Small,** *by Lynette Ranney Black, 128 pages, $19.95* Make your dream a reality. Analyze your needs and your space, then learn to plan and put it together. Lots of color photos!

5½ x 8½ BOOKS

☐ **Sew to Success!—How to Make Money in a Home-Based Sewing Business,** *by Kathleen Spike, 128 pgs., $10.95* Learn how to establish your market, set policies and procedures, price your talents and more!

☐ **Mother Pletsch's Painless Sewing,** *NEW Revised Edition, by Pati Palmer and Susan Pletsch, 128 pgs., $8.95* The most uncomplicated sewing book of the century! Filled with sewing tips on how to sew FAST!

Also available in spiralbound—$3.00 additional for large books, $2.00 for small.

☐ **Sewing With Sergers—The Complete Handbook for Overlock Sewing,** *Revised Edition, by Pati Palmer and Gail Brown, 128 pages, $8.95* Learn easy threading tips, stitch types, rolled edging and flat-locking on your serger.

☐ **Creative Serging—The Complete Handbook for Decorative Overlock Sewing,** *by Pati Palmer, Gail Brown and Sue Green, 128 pages, $8.95* In-depth information and creative uses of your serger.

☐ **Sensational Silk—A Handbook for Sewing Silk and Silk-like Fabrics,** *by Gail Brown, 128 pgs., $6.95* Complete guide for sewing with silk and silkies, plus all kinds of great blouse and dress techniques.

☐ **Pants For Any Body,** *Revised Edition, by Pati Palmer and Susan Pletsch, 128 pgs., $8.95* Learn to fit pants with clear step-by-step problem and solution illustrations.

☐ **Easy, Easier, Easiest Tailoring,** *Revised Edition, by Pati Palmer and Susan Pletsch, 128 pgs., $8.95* Learn 4 different tailoring methods, easy fit tips, and timesaving machine lining.

☐ **Clothes Sense—Straight Talk About Wardrobe Planning,** *by Barbara Weiland and Leslie Wood, 128 pgs., $6.95* Learn to define your personal style and when to sew or buy.

☐ **Sew a Beautiful Wedding,** *by Gail Brown and Karen Dillon, 128 pgs., $8.95* Bridal how-to's from choosing the most flattering style to sewing with specialty fabrics.

☐ **Decorating with Fabric: An Idea Book,** *by Judy Lindahl, 128 pgs., $6.95* Learn to cover walls, create canopies, valances, pillows, lamp shades, and more!

☐ **The Shade Book,** *Revised Edition, by Judy Lindahl, 152 pages, $9.95* Learn six major shade types, variations, trimmings, hardware, hemming, care, and upkeep.

☐ **Original Roo (The Purple Kangaroo),** *by Bob Benz, 48 pages, $5.95* A whimsical children's story about a kangaroo's adventures and how she saves the day with sewing.

Level I · Level II · Level III · Level IV

MY FIRST SEWING BOOK KITS

My First Sewing Books are packaged as kits, complete with materials for a first project. These kits, along with the Teaching Manual & Video offer a complete and thoroughly tested sewing program for young children. 5-to-11-year olds learn patience, manners, creativity, completion and how to follow rules...all through the enjoyment of sewing. Each book follows a project from start to finish with clever rhymes and clear illustrations. *Each book, 8½" x 8½", 40 pgs., $12.95*

☐ **My First Sewing Book,** *by Winky Cherry.* Children as young as 5 hand sew and stuff a felt bird shape. Also available in Spanish.

☐ **My First Embroidery Book,** *by Winky Cherry.* Beginners learn the importance of accuracy by making straight stitches, including the running and satin stitch, using a chart and gingham squares to make a name sampler.

☐ **My First Doll Book,** *by Winky Cherry.* These felt dolls have embroidered faces, yarn hair, and clothes. Children use the overstitch and embroidery skills learned in levels I and II.

☐ **My First Machine Sewing Book,** *by Winky Cherry.* With practice pages, then a fabric star, children learn about machine parts, seam allowances, tapering, snips, clips, stitching wrong sides out, and turning a shape right side out.

☐ **Teaching Children to Sew Manual and Video,** *$39.95* The 112-page, 8½" x 11" **Teaching Manual**, tells you exactly how to teach young children, including preparing the environment, workshop space, class control, and the importance of incorporating other life skills along with sewing skills. In the **Video**, see Winky Cherry teach six 6-to-8-year olds how to sew in a true-life classroom setting. Watch how she introduces herself and explains the rules and shows them how to sew. Then, see close-ups of a child sewing the project in double-time. This part could be shown to your students. Finally, Winky gives you a tour of an ideal classroom setup. She also talks about the tools, patterns and sewing supplies you will need.
1 hour.

☐ **Teacher's Starter Kit,** *$49.95* The refillable kit includes these hard-to-find items—a retail value of $73.00: 50 felt pieces in assorted colors (9 x 12"), 6 colors of crochet thread on balls, 2 packs of needles with large eyes, 2 pin cushions, 12 pre-cut birds, and printed patterns for shapes.

Deluxe Kits and additional classroom materials are available. Ask for our "As Easy As ABC" catalog.

VIDEOS

According to Robbie Fanning, author and critic, "The most professional of all the (video) tapes we've seen is Pati Palmer's *Sewing Today the Time Saving Way.* This tape should serve as the standard of excellence in the field." Following that standard, we have produced 8 more videos since Time Saving! *Videos are $29.95 each.*

☐ **Sewing Today the Time Saving Way,** 45 minutes featuring Lynn Raasch & Karen Dillon sharing tips and techniques to make sewing fun, fast and trouble free.

☐ **Sewing to Success!,** 45 minutes featuring Kathleen Spike who presents a wealth of information on how to achieve financial freedom working in your home as a professional dressmaker.

☐ **Sewing With Sergers—Basics,** 1 hour featuring Marta Alto & Pati Palmer on tensions, stitch types and their uses, serging circles, turning corners, gathering and much more.

☐ **Sewing With Sergers—Advanced,** 1 hour featuring Marta Alto & Pati Palmer on in-depth how-to's for rolled edging & flatlocking as well as garment details.

☐ **Creative Serging,** 1 hour featuring Marta Alto & Pati Palmer on how to use decorative threads, yarns and ribbons on your serger. PLUS: fashion shots!

☐ **Creative Serging II,** 1 hour featuring Marta Alto & Pati Palmer showing more creative ideas, including in-depth creative rolled edge.

☐ **Two-Hour Trousers,** 1 hour, 40 minutes, featuring Kathleen Spike with fit tips using our unique tissue fitting techniques, the best basics, and designer details.

☐ **Sewing Ultrasuede® Brand Fabrics—** Ultrasuede®, Facile®, Caress™, Ultra-leather™ 1 hour featuring Marta Alto and Pati Palmer with clear, step-by-step sewing demonstrations and fashion show.

☐ **Creative Home Decorating Ideas: Sewing Projects for the Home,** 1 hour featuring Lynette Ranney Black showing creative, easy ideas for windows, walls, tables and more. Companion to *Creative Serging for the Home.*

*An additional video from Palmer/Pletsch is available on **Teaching Children to Sew**, as part of a training package described on the previous page.*

TRENDS BULLETINS

Trends Bulletins are comprehensive 8-12 page two-color publications designed to keep you up-to-date by bringing you the best and the newest information on your favorite sewing topics.

☐ **The Newest in Sewing Room Design** *by Lynette Ranney Black.* This handbook for designing a sewing room covers proper sewing and pressing heights, layout styles, lighting and more. *$4.95*

☐ **Knitting Machines—An Introduction,** *by Terri Burns,* presents the basics of machine knitting, including stitch patterns, explanation of single and double bed machines, and a step-by-step guide to making your purchasing decision. *$3.95*

PALMER/PLETSCH WORKSHOPS

Our "Sewing Vacations" are offered on a variety of topics, including *Pant Fit, Fit, Tailoring, Creative Serging, Ultrasuede,* and a special *Best of Palmer/Pletsch* session. Workshops are held at the new Palmer/Pletsch International Training Center near the Portland, Oregon, airport. **Teacher training** sessions are also available on each topic. They include practice teaching sessions, hair styling, make-up and publicity photo session, up to 300 slides and script, camera-ready workbook handouts and publicity flyer and the manual **The BUSINE$$ of Teaching Sewing.** Call or write for schedules and information:

> Lynette Ranney Black, coordinator
> 1629 S. Eaden Road
> Oregon City, OR 97045
> (503) 631-7443

Palmer/Pletsch also carries hard-to-find and unique notions including Perfect Sew Wash-Away Fabric Stabilizer, Perfect Sew Needle Threader and decorative serging threads. Check your local fabric store or contact Palmer/Pletsch Publishing, P.O. Box 12046, Portland, OR 97212-0046. (503) 274-0687 or 1-800-728-3784 (order desk).